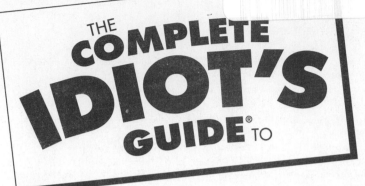

THE
COMPLETE
IDIOT'S
GUIDE® TO

Self-Testing Your Personality

by Arlene Matthews Uhl

ALPHA

A member of Penguin Group (USA) Inc.

ALPHA BOOKS

Published by the Penguin Group

Penguin Group (USA) Inc., 375 Hudson Street, New York, New York 10014, USA

Penguin Group (Canada), 90 Eglinton Avenue East, Suite 700, Toronto, Ontario M4P 2Y3, Canada (a division of Pearson Penguin Canada Inc.)

Penguin Books Ltd, 80 Strand, London WC2R 0RL, England

Penguin Ireland, 25 St. Stephen's Green, Dublin 2, Ireland (a division of Penguin Books Ltd.)

Penguin Group (Australia), 250 Camberwell Road, Camberwell, Victoria 3124, Australia (a division of Pearson Australia Group Pty. Ltd.)

Penguin Books India Pvt. Ltd., 11 Community Centre, Panchsheel Park, New Delhi—110 017, India

Penguin Group (NZ), 67 Apollo Drive, Rosedale, North Shore, Auckland 1311, New Zealand (a division of Pearson New Zealand Ltd.)

Penguin Books (South Africa) (Pty.) Ltd, 24 Sturdee Avenue, Rosebank, Johannesburg 2196, South Africa

Penguin Books Ltd., Registered Offices: 80 Strand, London WC2R 0RL, England

Copyright © 2008 by Arlene Matthews Uhl

THE COMPLETE IDIOT'S GUIDE TO and Design are registered trademarks of Penguin Group (USA) Inc.

International Standard Book Number: 978-1-59257-814-6
Library of Congress Catalog Card Number: 2008927331

10 09 08   8 7 6 5 4 3 2 1

Interpretation of the printing code: The rightmost number of the first series of numbers is the year of the book's printing; the rightmost number of the second series of numbers is the number of the book's printing. For example, a printing code of 08-1 shows that the first printing occurred in 2008.

Printed in the United States of America

Note: This publication contains the opinions and ideas of its author. It is intended to provide helpful and informative material on the subject matter covered. It is sold with the understanding that the author and publisher are not engaged in rendering professional services in the book. If the reader requires personal assistance or advice, a competent professional should be consulted.

The author and publisher specifically disclaim any responsibility for any liability, loss, or risk, personal or otherwise, which is incurred as a consequence, directly or indirectly, of the use and application of any of the contents of this book.

Most Alpha books are available at special quantity discounts for bulk purchases for sales promotions, premiums, fund-raising, or educational use. Special books, or book excerpts, can also be created to fit specific needs.

For details, write: Special Markets, Alpha Books, 375 Hudson Street, New York, NY 10014.

Publisher: *Marie Butler-Knight*
Editorial Director: *Mike Sanders*
Senior Managing Editor: *Billy Fields*
Acquisitions Editor: *Michele Wells*
Development Editor: *Lynn Northrup*
Production Editor: *Megan Douglass*

Copy Editor: *Jan Zoya*
Cartoonist: *Steve Barr*
Cover Designer: *Kurt Owens*
Book Designer: *Trina Wurst*
Layout: *Ayanna Lacey*
Proofreader: *Laura Caddell*

Contents

Introduction

If someone asked you to describe yourself, a long list of adjectives might come to mind. You might think of yourself as extroverted or shy, as an optimist or a pessimist, as a daredevil or a cautious type. You might describe yourself as generous or funny or "a great listener" or a "natural leader." Here's your chance to put your self-evaluations to the test—or, more specifically, to many tests.

In the pages of *The Complete Idiot's Guide to Self-Testing Your Personality*, you'll have dozens of opportunities to learn more about yourself, to identify prevalent patterns in your actions and attitudes, and to unearth aspects of yourself you may not have thought much about before. This entertaining and illuminating process of getting better acquainted with yourself can be the beginning of a new level of self-awareness that can help you be the best "you" you can be.

The Complete Idiot's Guide to Self-Testing Your Personality is a strictly "for fun" collection of self-assessments. Don't worry: these are not the kind of tests you can fail. They're meant to get you thinking and to whet your appetite for even more self-discovery. They also make great ice-breakers and conversation starters if you are willing to share and compare your results with those of your friends, co-workers, or loved ones.

These quizzes are simple and straightforward. They're "easy" in the sense that they're about one of your favorite subjects: you. However, there is one important caveat. All of the tests rely on you to report about yourself. Be as honest as possible as you respond to the questions. If you're not, the only person you'll be cheating is yourself.

Finally, remember that there is certainly no ideal or "perfect" personality. Most of our personal characteristics have accompanying advantages and disadvantages. Learning about the things that make you the completely unique individual that you are can help you make the most of each and every day.

How This Book Is Organized

This book is divided into six parts:

Part 1, "What's My Style?," offers quizzes on some basic personality components. It helps you evaluate whether you are an extrovert or an introvert, an optimist or a pessimist. It also offers measures for your levels of creativity, your assertiveness, your risk tolerance, and your self-confidence. These quintessential characteristics are likely to influence many aspects of your work life, your love life, and your social life.

Part 2, "My Personality at Work," takes a closer look at factors of your personality that could potentially impact your career path and job success. In this section you'll find measures of your leadership skills, your entrepreneurial potential, and your team skills. You'll also find out how good an interview you are and how strong a speaker you are.

Part 3, "My Personality in Love and Marriage," offers measures of some key relationship skills, such as your ability to be considerate and to keep your head during disagreements. It also looks at how romantic you are, how sensual you are, and how sex savvy you are.

Part 4, "My Personality with Friends, Neighbors, and Others," hones in on your social traits. It includes assessments of your affability, your sense of humor, your generosity, and your empathy. It even includes a quiz that tells you if you are more suited to feline or canine companionship.

Part 5, "My Money Personality," helps you evaluate your inclinations when it comes to saving, spending, and investing those hard-earned dollars. You'll learn whether your head or your heart rules your money decisions, whether you have a tendency to be careless with money, and whether or not you're likely to be driven by money envy.

Part 6, "My People-Wise Personality," evaluates your interpersonal and intrapersonal intelligence. You'll find out how good you are at understanding others, including whether you're skilled at decoding body language and spotting liars. You'll also learn something about your level of insight into your own emotional traits.

A Note About Scoring

Each personality quiz will explain the method you should use for scoring. There is no rocket science involved here. However, just to avoid any confusion, I'd like to acquaint you with a common psychological testing concept known as *reverse scoring*, which some of the quizzes will incorporate.

When the instructions tell you to reverse a score, you will trade the highest-possible scores for the lowest-possible scores, and vice versa. This is to streamline the test and keep test-takers from trying to "guess" which responses will lead to which outcomes.

For example, a test trying to determine if you are a risk-taker might ask you to assign a number to statements indicating whether or not you agree with them:

---

1. Strongly disagree

2. Somewhat disagree

3. Feel neutral or are not sure

4. Somewhat agree

5. Strongly agree

Two of the test questions might read:

I'm likely to take an "adventure" vacation.

I would never consider bungee jumping.

An extreme risk-taker would likely assign a "5" to the first statement, and a "1" to the second. If high scores are meant to indicate a propensity for risk-taking, reversing the score for the second item would yield the correct result. In the instructions that accompany each test, you will be told which items—if any—require reverse scoring, and you'll be reminded how to do it.

Trademarks

All terms mentioned in this book that are known to be or are suspected of being trademarks or service marks have been appropriately capitalized. Alpha Books and Penguin Group (USA) Inc. cannot attest to the accuracy of this information. Use of a term in this book should not be regarded as affecting the validity of any trademark or service mark.

Part 1

What's My Style?

Do you thrive in—or in front of—a crowd, or do you prefer your own company? Is your glass half full, or does your cup runneth over with optimism? Do you stand up for yourself, or have a tendency to knuckle under? You might think you know the answers to these and other essential personality questions, but in the first part of this book, you put your assumptions to the test.

WELL, I JUST TOOK A PERSONALITY TEST, AND APPARENTLY, YOU WERE RIGHT. I AM A **PIG!**

BARR

Am I Outgoing?

Some of us are the "life of the party," some would rather have a root canal than attend a party, and some fall in between these polar opposites. It takes all kinds to make the world spin, but virtually all psychologists who study personality agree that whether we are extroverted or introverted is a key personality trait; it influences many practical aspects of our lives, including our career paths, relationships, and self-image.

Are you sociable and fun-loving, or more introspective and reserved? Do you take greater pleasure in group activities, or do you prefer solitary pursuits? By taking this test, you'll learn about your predominant tendencies and how they help to define you.

Keep in mind that all of us can think of situations where we might behave in a way that is opposed to our usual manner. For example, even an extrovert may hold back to some extent in an unfamiliar and highly formal social situation, while she scopes out proper protocols (such as, is it all right to high-five the Queen of England?). And even an extreme introvert may edge toward expansiveness (albeit perhaps not so happily) in a situation where not being convivial (say, the boss's annual holiday party) would be considered rude, inappropriate, and even self-destructive. But as you answer these questions, try to respond in terms of your prevalent disposition—that is, note the way you usually act and feel. That will help you understand the aspects of your personality that are most enduring and therefore most influential over time.

Take the Test

Pick the letter that applies to you:

1. Your typical response to a party invitation is ...

    A. Oh boy!

    B. I'll consider it.

    C. Oh no!

2. The likelihood that you will throw a party in the next 12 months is ...

    A. Nearly 100 percent.

    B. About 50/50.

    C. Less than zero.

3. If a camera were to follow you to a large social gathering, where would it be most likely to pan in on you?

    A. In the center of the room surrounded by other people

    B. Milling about near the refreshments

    C. Hugging the walls

4. An acquaintance invites you to join a book club discussion group. You ...

    A. Agree enthusiastically, and rush out to get the book they're currently reading.

    B. Ask who's in the group and what kinds of books they prefer.

    C. Decline. You love reading because it is a *solitary* activity.

5. You are sitting at a sushi bar between two strangers. You will …

   A. Initiate a conversation about the food or weather or any common ground.

   B. Be open to conversation if someone else starts it.

   C. Refuse to say so much as, "Please pass the soy sauce."

6. A business dinner is cancelled at the last minute, and you find yourself facing an unexpected evening alone. You …

   A. Call everyone you know to see who's free.

   B. Say "oh well" and think of something you can do around the house.

   C. Are happy as a kitten in a yarn factory.

7. You board an airplane for a cross-country flight, and your seatmate asks where you're headed and what you'll do when you get there. You …

   A. Eagerly get into a five-hour conversation.

   B. Respond politely, and then use body language to indicate you'd rather sleep or watch the movie.

   C. Consider jumping out the window at 35,000 feet.

8. Your boss announces that someone in your department will be given a promotion that involves additional selling and other customer contact. You …

   A. Enthusiastically campaign for the job.

   B. Weigh all the pros and cons of the position, regardless of how you feel about its increased social aspect.

   C. Hide behind your computer screen.

9. How likely are you to express strong emotions, such as joy, anger, or sorrow, around others?

   A. You wear your heart on your sleeve.

   B. You are apt to do so in front of those you are close to.

   C. As likely as your pet rock.

10. For you, going to the movies alone is …

    A. An unthinkable prospect.

    B. An occasional opportunity to eat an entire bag of popcorn.

    C. Heaven.

11. You would be most likely to engage in the following games:

    A. Twister/charades

    B. Scrabble/Monopoly

    C. Solitaire/anything on your Nintendo DS

12. For you, the idea of learning to calmly and quietly meditate is …

    A. Absolutely ridiculous.

    B. An interesting but unlikely prospect.

    C. Appealing.

13. In how many community, social, or volunteer organizations do you actively participate?

    A. More than three

    B. Two or three

    C. One or none

14. How likely would you be to ask a question during a Q&A session following a speaker presentation?

    A. Extremely likely.

    B. I would if I had a really good question.

    C. Not on your life.

15. What is the likelihood you would offer to *give* a speaker presentation?

    A. Very high.

    B. I would if I were really needed.

    C. Yeah, right.

Scoring and Explanation

Assign yourself 3 points for every "A" response, 2 points for every "B" response, and 1 point for every "C" response. Tally your points:

♦ **A score of 40–45** indicates that you are highly outgoing—an *extrovert*. For you, gratification comes primarily from interactions with the outside world. Talkative and enthusiastic, you take pleasure in group activities and social gatherings. You are unafraid to express yourself in public. You are a joiner and a potential leader.

Extroverts generally report relatively high levels of personal happiness. However, one caveat you might bear in mind is that because you draw so much of your energy from other people, you might tend toward lethargy and boredom when alone. Remember that you can be good company to yourself as well as to others. Consider stepping off the social treadmill once in a while and getting reacquainted with *you*.

♦ **A score of 25–39** indicates that you are somewhat outgoing—an *ambivert*. Extroversion and introversion are ends of a continuum. Your scores are near the midway mark. Ambiversion is the term used to describe people like you, who can exhibit tendencies shown by both extroverts and introverts. As an ambivert, you are generally comfortable in groups and enjoy social interaction—even if you are not "the star of the show." However, you also appreciate time alone and breaks from the hubbub of the crowd. All in all, you manifest a nice balance.

♦ **A score of 15–24** indicates that you are not very outgoing—an *introvert*. You are reserved, reflective, and self-reliant. You do not make friends easily, although you may certainly have a small number of valued and trusted friends. You primarily draw energy from and take pleasure in solitary activities. You could be very creative—excelling in an endeavor such as writing, painting, composing, or even computer programming.

Many people think of all introverts as shy. But shyness indicates a discomfort with social situations. You might be shy, but you might simply *prefer* your own company much of the time. It would also be wrong to characterize you as antisocial. As the famously introverted Woody Allen has said, "I am not antisocial. I am just not social."

2

How Optimistic Am I?

It seems like optimists have all the fun. Although life cycles through ups and downs for both optimists and pessimists, an impressive body of research shows that optimists react to events in ways that promote their emotional and physical well-being. Their "look on the bright side" dispositions help them manage stress, cope creatively with challenges, maintain supportive relationships, and recover more quickly from setbacks. As if that's not enough, optimists tend to stay healthier and live longer than their pessimistic counterparts. (Sorry, I know this bit of knowledge might make any pessimists out there even gloomier than you were before.)

But psychologists now say it's possible to be *too* optimistic. Like most extreme attitudes, extreme optimism can create problems of its own. Being wildly optimistic, for example, can translate into being wildly impractical and imprudent.

Optimism and pessimism are two ends of a continuum. Researchers note that about 80 percent of the U.S. population is distributed from mildly to unremittingly optimistic. Take the following quiz to find out just how optimistic you are, and what that might mean for the way your future unfolds.

Take the Test

Pick the letter that applies to you:

1. You and several colleagues are competing for a promotion at work, and someone else lands it. You …

   A. Tell yourself you will never get ahead.

   B. Think back on all the times you've lost out on an opportunity.

   C. Promise yourself you'll work harder to get the next promotion that comes along.

   D. Quit immediately, confident you will find a better job where your obvious talents will be appreciated.

2. At the last minute, you ask someone you really like out on a Saturday-night date. She says she's sorry but she's already made plans. You …

   A. Mope all night while listening to blues music on your iPod.

   B. Assume you will end up old and alone.

   C. Decide to ask the same person again on Monday if she wants to go out the following Saturday night.

   D. Decide to ask the same person out again next Saturday for that night, hoping she won't be busy then.

3. You lead a campaign to win a new client's business, but the client signs with a competing firm. You …

   A. Rush off to the restroom and make the "L" hand sign for "loser" on your forehead as you stare into the mirror.

   B. Assume you're going to get demoted or fired.

   C. Tell yourself it's the client's loss.

   D. Tell the client it's his loss and assure him he'll be back begging to work with you.

4. You sign up to take a challenging course and fail the first test. You …

   A. Drop the course because it is obviously over your head.

   B. Tell yourself you're a hopeless dunce.

   C. Promise yourself to study harder for the next test.

   D. Assume you'll do better next time, but don't set aside time to do any additional studying.

5. You come home to find a notice in your mailbox saying there is a certified letter for you at the post office. You …

   A. Stay awake all night wondering what bad news the letter brings.

   B. Assume someone is suing you, and you call your friends asking for the name of a good lawyer.

   C. Make a mental note to pick it up tomorrow, and then you get on with your usual activities.

   D. Tell yourself it's probably some sort of nonsense and decide not to pick up the letter.

6. You just got a really bad haircut. You …

   A. Tell yourself you're going to look awful for a long time.

   B. Cancel as many social plans as possible.

   C. Wear a hat and a smile.

   D. Dye your hair green, assuming this will detract attention from your haircut.

7. You interview for a very competitive job, and you are hired from a large pool of qualified applicants. You …

   A. Feel like you just got lucky for some inexplicable reason.

   B. Worry that you'll soon fail and be discovered as a fraud.

   C. Pat yourself on the back for your solid qualifications and interview skills.

   D. Turn the job down, because if you can land this great a job, you can land an even better one.

8. You win $10,000 in the state lottery! You ...

   A. Refuse to spend any of it until you verify numerous times that it is not a mistake.

   B. Refuse to spend any of it because you assume now something bad—and very costly—will occur.

   C. Save some, spend some, and buy another lottery ticket next month.

   D. Head to Las Vegas where you hope to double your money.

9. At a party, someone attractive smiles at you from across the room. You ...

   A. Look behind you to see who it is he's *really* smiling at.

   B. Tell yourself he must be smiling at you out of pity because you feel so uncomfortable and look so out of place.

   C. Smile back and casually move in his direction.

   D. Gather your friends around and brag that the attractive person over there is gaga over you.

10. You're selected from a live television program to get a free makeover. You ...

   A. Tell yourself it's because you're so unattractive.

   B. Decline because you assume the makeover will be a failure.

   C. Accept because you think it will be fun and you might get some good tips.

   D. Assume this is the day you will be discovered by a major talent scout.

11. After anxiously awaiting the results of a serious medical test, you learn that the test is negative. You are fine. You ...

   A. Tell yourself you've dodged a bullet—*for now*.

   B. Worry that the test results are mistaken.

   C. Celebrate.

   D. Vow never to get a medical checkup again because doctors just scare you over nothing.

12. You embark on a weight-loss diet. After a month of exercising and watching what you eat, you lose the 10 pounds you wanted to shed. You …

   A. Think about how hard the past month was and how deprived you felt.

   B. Tell yourself you'll never keep the weight off.

   C. Pat yourself on the back and vow to maintain your new weight.

   D. Go back to your old habits, assuming you've permanently changed your metabolism.

13. When you think back on your life so far, you …

   A. Think mostly about failures and disappointments.

   B. Think mostly about missed opportunities and roads not taken.

   C. Think mostly about positive events and relationships.

   D. Not applicable! You refuse to think about the past—life is all about moving forward.

14. After adverse events in your life, you …

   A. Take a long time to feel like yourself again.

   B. Withdraw from friends and social activities.

   C. Take some time to regroup, then come back stronger.

   D. Take an immediate "get back on the horse" approach.

15. Which statement do you most agree with?

   A. Whatever can go wrong, will go wrong.

   B. If it were raining soup, I'd only have a fork.

   C. Things usually turn out for the best.

   D. Life is just a bowl of cherries—minus the pits!

Scoring and Explanation

Assign yourself 1 point for every "A" or "B" response, 2 points for every "C" response, and 3 points for every "D" response. Tally your points:

◆ **A score of 15–24** indicates that you are a pessimist. When something goes wrong, you tend to assume that *everything* will *always* go wrong. You have difficulty keeping your negative reactions from spreading. You also tend to feel relatively powerless to impact the course of events. The bad news is that your habitual sense of helplessness might itself be the cause of some of your difficulties. Attitudes fuel your actions, and actions contribute to outcomes. If you don't believe you can accomplish something, chances are you won't be able to. But the good news—if you can stand to hear some good news—is that pessimism is a cognitive habit that can be broken.

Developing self-awareness about your habitual reactions to events is a first step on the road to change. The second is overhauling your *explanatory style*. Notice when you leap to the conclusion that a temporary problem will last forever, or that a difficulty in one area of your life will spread to other areas. Remind yourself that such conclusions are unproven and most likely illogical. With time and practice you can learn to stop catastrophizing.

◆ **A score of 25–34** indicates that you are an optimist. When things are going poorly, you assume they will change for the better sooner or later. You remain alert to positive elements in negative situations, and you accept challenges and limitations while holding on to hope. When your life is going well, you're not afraid to enjoy it.

Best of all, your score indicates you are a *realistic optimist*. You are capable of performing reality checks, know how to exercise forethought, and have good old common sense. You don't just hope for the best; you contribute to making positive things happen.

◆ **A score of 35–45** indicates that you could be an unrealistic optimist. Your high score indicates that your optimism contains at least some elements of carelessness. At times, you can be so relentlessly upbeat that you deny reality. When this occurs, you could be in jeopardy of leaving too much to chance and failing to put into motion the very plans that could make your dreams come true.

All optimists are a bit biased in a self-serving way, and to a certain extent, this tends to work out well. But you underestimate risk to such a large degree that it could be hazardous. Researchers are now suggesting that there may be an *optimal margin of illusion* that enables people to slightly overestimate chances of success; however, that does not typically lead to irresponsible behaviors based on false assumptions. See if you can curb your enthusiasm a bit so that you can fall within that margin. Optimism and realism need not be mutually exclusive. It's fine to take a calculated risk, but resist plunging headlong into uncertain situations without a little research and rumination.

3

Do I Like *Me?*

Are you confident in your abilities? Do you believe you can accomplish what you set out to do? Do you think your presence is desirable? Above all, are you comfortable with who you are, even if you're not strictly "perfect"?

Self-regard is related to many areas of psychological functioning. It affects your overall life adjustment, your satisfaction in relationships, and your performance in many kinds of endeavors. Take the following quiz to learn about your self-image and self-regard—in short, to discover just how much you like yourself.

Take the Test

For each of the following statements, indicate the number of the statement that corresponds to your level of agreement or disagreement:

1. Strongly disagree

2. Somewhat disagree

3. Feel neutral or are not sure

4. Somewhat agree

5. Strongly agree

1. I often find myself wishing I were someone else.

2. I can hold my own in almost any conversation.

3. I often have good ideas.

4. I fear failing at new endeavors.

5. I can cope with whatever comes my way.

6. I am physically attractive.

7. I fear others say negative things about me behind my back.

8. I enjoy my own company.

9. I withhold my opinions for fear I'll look stupid.

10. I often feel like a misfit—a square peg in a round hole.

11. I am never boring.

12. I am a good person, even if I make some mistakes.

13. I often feel ashamed of my thoughts.

14. If I fail at something, I blame circumstances rather than myself.

15. I am able and eager to learn new things.

16. People enjoy talking to me.

17. I make a good first impression.

18. Any success of mine is dumb luck.

19. I often get frustrated with my shortcomings.

20. Deep down, I'm not a very nice person.

21. I can make people laugh (*with* me, not *at* me).

22. I am embarrassed about my age.

23. I'm sexy.

24. There's a big gap between who I'd like to be and who I am.

25. I often feel proud of my work.

26. I give up easily.

27. I'm popular.

28. I enhance the lives of the people I interact with.

29. I can rely on myself.

30. I accept my flaws.

31. I am lovable.

32. Most people can convince me to change my mind.

33. I often feel like a phony.

34. Many people would like to be more like me.

35. I find it easy to accept a compliment.

36. I get better as I get older.

37. The list of things I'd change about myself is long.

38. Most criticism does not upset me.

39. I keep many secrets about myself.

40. If one thing goes wrong in my life, I don't let it ruin my day.

41. I often wish I had more energy.

42. I have a "can do" attitude.

43. I wish I could control my emotions better.

44. I learn from my mistakes.

45. I often have fun.

46. When I feel discouraged I eat or drink too much.

47. I can generally achieve whatever I set my mind to.

48. I have a special talent or ability.

49. A list of my good qualities would be very long.

50. My funeral would be well attended, the eulogies would be filled with glowing stories about me, and mourners would cry their eyes out!

Scoring and Explanation

Before tallying your total points, be sure to *reverse the score* (5 = 1, 4 = 2, 3 = 3, 2 = 4, 1 = 5) *for the following items:* 1, 4, 7, 9, 10, 13, 18, 19, 20, 22, 24, 26, 32, 33, 37, 39, 41, 43, 46. Remember, in reversing the score, high numbers are traded for low and vice versa. Unless you reverse the scores for the items listed—and *only* for the items listed— your result will be inaccurate. See the Introduction to this book for a full explanation of reverse scoring.

Tally your points:

◆ **A score of 50–150** indicates that you are far from being your own best friend. You have a low level of self-confidence and self-regard. It's possible that a significant person in your past disparaged you, or, conversely, that someone continually told you how magnificent you were without regard to what you actually accomplished. Either type of message could have contributed to your self-doubt. Whatever the reason, you will take a great deal more satisfaction from life if you stop being so self-critical. If you have gone so far as to complete this test, then you have it within you to take the first steps toward increased self-regard. The most important thing to remember is that you do not have to be flawless to be valuable. The key to healthy self-regard lies not in an overly inflated ego, but rather in a willingness to accept yourself as the multifaceted being that you are.

◆ **A score of 151–174** indicates that you struggle with self-doubts in various areas. You could benefit from giving yourself a few pep talks, and from actively recalling actions you took that led to successes in your life. Think, too, about the people who care about you. They obviously see positive characteristics in you, so try to look at yourself from their perspective. Make a list of, and review, your strengths. If, after doing so, you are left with some things you want to change, then take the initiative to change them. The fact that you've been motivated enough to take this quiz means you have the capacity to be proactive.

◆ **A score of 175–199** indicates that you have a fairly high level of self-regard. Although you might want to reexamine a few insecurities, you generally like and feel comfortable with yourself—warts and all. That means that others tend to like you and feel comfortable around you as well. Your level of self-confidence should help you to reach your goals, and help you to keep setting and attaining new goals.

◆ **A score of 200–250** indicates that *you* and *you* are BFFs (best friends forever). You have a high level of self-regard that should help you succeed in most areas of life. It will also serve to keep you positive and resilient, even in the face of setbacks. One thing to look out for is this: if you are at the very high end of this group (235 and over), be sure that you are not engaging in defensive self-regard, i.e., denying the fact that you are less than perfect in any way. That kind of extreme attitude can set you up for a fall. A touch of humility might be in order.

4

Am I a Risk-Taker?

Risk-taking behavior, or the lack thereof, is a fundamental personality trait. Some people rate very high in this characteristic and carry it across all areas of their lives. For them, life is never a dull moment. At the other end of the spectrum are people for whom prudence itself is a passion. They don't like the idea of stepping outside their box—they like their box very much, thank you.

Do you typically throw caution to the wind, or do you prefer the "warm blanket" feeling of the safe and the familiar? There's no time like the present to find out. Go ahead: take the risk.

Take the Test

For each of the following statements, indicate the number of the statement that corresponds to your experience with or feeling about the activity:

1. Would never consider it
2. Might consider it
3. Would seriously consider it
4. Have already done it

1. Take a vacation by myself
2. Quit a job without having another lined up
3. Ask someone on a date without formally meeting the person first
4. Drive over the speed limit
5. Gamble in a casino
6. Sing karaoke in a public place
7. Visit a fortune-teller
8. Get a tattoo
9. Try a very different haircut
10. Take in a stray animal
11. Give a ride to a stranger in apparent need
12. Ride in a small airplane
13. Skydive
14. Hike trails without a map
15. Bungee jump
16. Scuba dive

17. Visit a place where I don't speak the language and few people speak mine

18. Enter a talent show

19. Do a stand-up comedy routine

20. Volunteer for a magician's act

21. Attend a party where I don't know anyone

22. Introduce myself to someone famous

23. Try an entirely unfamiliar cuisine

24. Surf

25. Snowboard

26. Wear an outrageous Halloween costume

27. Play a practical joke

28. Throw a surprise party

29. Apply for a job I'm not really qualified for

30. Go back to school as an adult

31. Change careers entirely

32. Enter a contest to ride the space shuttle

33. Camp out by myself

34. Sail a long distance in a small boat

35. Go on a jungle safari

36. Go whitewater rafting

37. Take flying lessons

38. Buy a hot stock on a tip

39. Have children

40. Go on *Deal or No Deal*

Scoring and Explanation

To obtain your score, simply tally your points for each item:

◆ **A score of 136–160** indicates that you thrive on risk. You enjoy the thrill of seeking physical sensations and putting yourself on the line emotionally. For you, living without adventure is not really living. You may be very susceptible to boredom if you are not seeking out some new adventure or shaking things up in your life. As with most things, risk-taking has its pluses and minuses. Hopefully you are channeling your love of excitement into productive new challenges most of the time. If you are simply seeking sensation for its own sake, without heed to long-term goals or without any prudent checks and balances, you could end up in the danger zone.

◆ **A score of 101–135** indicates that you enjoy a moderate level of risk. You're no daredevil, but you'll take a chance on something now and then—maybe just for the fun of it, or maybe because you are just fed up with sameness. If all your risk-taking is centered in one area—for example, sports—know that you probably do have the capacity to transfer your boldness to another area as well. Perhaps you'll ultimately want to try some new intellectual endeavor, or consider something that will jump-start your career.

◆ **A score of 100 or below** suggests you like to play it safe. You probably like to feel "in control," and you certainly do not care for surprises. Others probably don't find you very surprising, either. (You can verify this by taking Quiz #5, *How Predictable Am I?*) But consider, when your life is drawing to a close, it might well be the things you *haven't* tried that you'll regret. For now, you might be energized, even rejuvenated, by taking just a wee chance or two. It's unlikely you are apt to strap on a parachute (unless you routinely do so as a precaution when cleaning out your rain gutters), but think about some baby steps you can take to get your blood racing every once in a while.

5

How Predictable Am I?

Do your friends and family know what you're going to say before you say it? Can your co-workers set their watches by observing what you're doing at any given time of day? Does your dog stand at the door in happy anticipation of a walk, knowing he'll be gratified at precisely the same moment each morning and evening? If so, you're reliable and dependable. That's good—to a point. Stability can generate a certain amount of calm and satisfaction. Without it, life can be a case of "follow the bouncing ball."

But if the above describes you to a fault, your life could be devoid of spontaneity. Perhaps that won't be so satisfying to you in the long run. Stepping outside of your comfort zone once in a while can be exciting and energizing. Participating in new activities can actually stimulate the release of feel-good chemicals in your brain. You wouldn't want to miss out on that—or would you?

Take the following test to see how predictable you really are.

Take the Test

For each of the following statements, indicate the number of the statement that corresponds to your level of agreement or disagreement:

---

1. Strongly disagree

2. Somewhat disagree

3. Feel neutral or are not sure

4. Somewhat agree

5. Strongly agree

---

1. I can tell you with a high degree of certainty what I'll be doing for the next four Saturday nights.

2. If someone I liked sent me an unexpected party invitation for one of those four Saturday nights, I'd probably change my plans and go.

3. I rarely skip a meal or eat between meals.

4. I am a registered member of a political party, and I unfailingly vote for a member of that party.

5. Even if I have a strong opinion, I can be swayed to the other side of an issue by a sound argument.

6. I can easily find any item in my office.

7. I can easily locate any item in my house.

8. I would love to be given a surprise party.

9. I go to bed at the same time each night.

10. I enjoy watching pilots for new television shows.

11. If a new restaurant opened in town, I'd be among the first to try it.

12. When I cook from a recipe, I am unlikely to add or change any ingredients.

13. I have seen or would like to see a theatrical production in previews.

14. I shop for clothes out of necessity rather than out of wanting to update my wardrobe.

15. I have trouble sleeping in strange beds.

16. I hate mysteries.

17. I love puzzles.

18. I dread having to learn how to use a new technology.

19. I am great at remembering birthdays, anniversaries, and other significant dates.

20. Most people who know me find me easy to buy gifts for.

21. I prefer fiction to nonfiction.

22. I could easily give an extemporaneous talk.

23. I don't mind watching reruns on TV.

24. I would rather have too much information than not enough.

25. I would never cancel plans I'd committed to, except in a genuine emergency.

26. On occasion, I have "played hooky" from school or work.

27. I routinely seek out long-range weather reports.

28. I love getting a new appliance or gadget.

29. When I take a vacation, I tend to revisit places I've already been.

30. My taste in music is very eclectic.

31. I would be very reluctant to try any type of alternative medical treatment, even if people whom I trusted vouched that it did wonders.

32. I enjoy observing holiday traditions.

33. I get bored when things stay the same for too long.

34. I always go grocery shopping with a list and stick to that list.

35. I do not like to answer the phone unless I know who's calling.

36. I enjoy pursuing self-improvement.

37. I have given the same type of gift to numerous people.

38. I'd love to take a class in something I know very little about.

39. I've fantasized about what it would be like to live in another time period.

40. If I thought I saw a flying saucer, I'd tell myself there was a logical explanation and forget about it.

Scoring and Explanation

Before tallying your total points, be sure to *reverse the score* (5 = 1, 4 = 2, 3 = 3, 2 = 4, 1 = 5) *for the following items*: 2, 5, 8, 10, 11, 13, 17, 21, 22, 24, 26, 28, 30, 33, 36, 38, 39. Remember, in reversing the score, high numbers are traded for low and vice versa. Unless you reverse the scores for the items listed—and *only* for the items listed—your result will be inaccurate. See the Introduction to this book for a full explanation of reverse scoring.

Tally your points:

◆ **A score of 40–79** indicates that you are not very predictable, except in the sense that you can be predicted to be unpredictable. It could be said that you're something of a wild card. You can be very spontaneous, perhaps even impulsive at times. While it's certainly true that you relish new and unique experiences, it's worth mentioning that you might be spreading yourself a bit thin. Don't be afraid to explore some things in-depth, as that can provide as much pleasure as dabbling in the unfamiliar. You're eager to discover what you might like; however, once you know you like something, don't forget to take some time to savor it.

◆ **A score of 80–119** indicates that you are predictable in some ways, but that in other ways you can definitely be spontaneous and adventurous. Although your affinity for the unique and unexpected does not apply to every area of your life, there is

enough newness in your day-to-day experience to keep you interested and to make you a very interesting person who can keep
others guessing.

◆ **A score of 120–159** indicates that you are fairly predictable across
the board. Although you're not afraid to step out of your box once
in a great while, you essentially feel most comfortable when you
arrange your life to include few surprises and shake-ups. It probably wouldn't hurt you to shake things up a bit. You'd be surprised
how much fun a surprise can be.

◆ **A score of 160–200** indicates that you are as predictable as the
tides. You are motivated to avoid new experiences, even if they are
potentially pleasurable. You dislike being exposed to new information and technology, even if those things might ultimately make
your life easier. You'd rather be bored than challenged, and you
make choices accordingly. You should be aware, however, that
most people who describe themselves as very happy in life typically
pursue fresh new experiences on a regular basis. Your *neophobia*—
fear of the new—could potentially hold you back from experiencing a life filled with meaning and purpose. Of course, the best-laid
plans—yes, even yours—might take an unexpected direction. Your
attitude might shift on its own as your life evolves. Perhaps a new
job or parenthood or some other major development will jolt you
out of your complacent state.

What's My Stress Style?

Some stressful situations are unavoidable. We all have days when no amount of power, planning, money, or luck can protect us from being on the receiving end of life's little bombshells. Stuff happens, as they say, but it's how we *react* to that stuff that separates the frustrated and frazzled from the patient and peaceful.

When things go wrong, or even when we suspect they *could possibly* go wrong, we each respond in our own style. Some of us may grow angry or aggressive. Some of us will do our best to shrug off our frustrations and make the best of our circumstances.

What's your stress style? You probably have a hunch already. But here's a quiz to help you learn more.

Take the Test

Imagine yourself in the following circumstances and select which of the two reactions you'd be most likely to have:

1. You've spent hours at the office writing up an important report on your desktop; then you accidentally delete it from your computer. You …

   A. Slam your fist into your desk and swear before frantically starting over.

   B. Call your IT department, explain your dilemma, and ask them to help you try to retrieve your work.

2. You are in your car waiting for your turn at a drive-through bank window. The person in the car ahead of you is having a lengthy chat with the teller. You …

   A. Lean on your horn and point at your watch.

   B. Flip through your car radio channels for a song you like.

3. Your new puppy has an accident on your Oriental rug. You …

   A. Holler at him and blame your family for talking you into getting a puppy.

   B. Get out the carpet cleaner—and leave it out for the next time.

4. Your 16-year-old son slams his bedroom door while you're nagging him. You …

   A. Open the door, keep nagging, and then slam it yourself.

   B. Take some time to cool down, and try to think of an effective way to get through to him.

5. Your usually nice boss yells at you for no good reason. You …

   A. Yell back, and then complain loudly to anyone who will listen.

   B. Assume he's having a bad day.

6. You're stuck in a traffic jam that looks as if it might last for hours. You ...

   A. Wedge your vehicle onto the shoulder of the road and try to pass other vehicles.

   B. Call home to say you'll be late, and then pop an audio book into your CD player.

7. You're on a committee that seems to be getting nowhere in making a decision. You ...

   A. Storm out of the meeting, protesting the group's inefficiency.

   B. Try to think of compromises that might lead to a consensus.

8. You're in the midst of a disagreement. You ...

   A. Keep raising your voice as the debate goes on.

   B. Modulate your voice so as not to escalate the conflict.

9. You are working on a tough problem with an extremely tight deadline. You ...

   A. Drink a lot of coffee and cut back on sleep.

   B. Sleep on the problem and hope this will help you come up with a creative solution.

10. The person ahead of you on a 10-items-or-less grocery store checkout line has 15 items. You ...

    A. Point this out with great exasperation.

    B. Take the opportunity to flip through the *National Enquirer* with guilty pleasure.

11. You get distracted while cooking a family dinner, and you burn the meal beyond recognition. You ...

    A. Fling the dinner into the sink and angrily ask why no one else ever cooks dinner.

    B. Order pizza.

12. You open an unsettling piece of mail at night and can't reach its sender until morning. You …

    A. Stew all night, rehearsing what you'll say over and over.

    B. Take a warm bath to help you get to sleep.

13. Your home Internet server goes down. You …

    A. Immediately rush off to a Starbucks and log onto their wireless network.

    B. Start an activity that doesn't require Internet access.

14. You call a customer service hotline and are put on hold. You …

    A. Furiously hang up, and then realize you have to start all over.

    B. Put the call on speakerphone and do something else until a human comes on the line.

15. You must read a document and can't find your reading glasses. You …

    A. Run around like a headless chicken, repeatedly asking who has hidden your reading glasses.

    B. Ask someone to read the document to you, and then make a note to stock up on extra spectacles.

Scoring and Explanation

Count up your number of "A" responses and "B" responses:

◆ **A total of between 11 and 15 "A" answers** indicates that your habitual reaction to stress is high. You have what is known in psychological parlance as a "Type A" stress style. You tend to be very irritated by relatively trivial events, are impatient with others and with yourself, and are easily angered when your goals are thwarted. When pressure is present, you speed up—even if this is counterproductive to what you are trying to accomplish. In general, you live in a perennial state of "combat readiness," reacting with aggression when you feel threatened.

Pure Type As are relatively rare, but if this describes you, you should take steps to adjust your attitude or you could potentially jeopardize your health. Studies show that Type A individuals can be at risk for cardiovascular problems, as well as a number of other illnesses that have been associated to some degree with negative stress—including colds, headaches, and stomach disorders.

Chill out and slow down. Try to view people with different approaches to life than yours—who perhaps do things more slowly and methodically—as role models from whom you can learn something, rather than as pains in your neck.

◆ **A total of between 8 and 10 "A" answers** indicates that your habitual reaction to stress is moderately high. You are a moderate Type A. While not every setback or frustration pushes your buttons, plenty of things can upset you to the point where you are potentially hurting yourself. Notice what tiny irritants tend to set off an enormous stress reaction, and ask yourself which is likely to harm you more: the minor annoyance or your major upset. It's all about perspective.

◆ **A total of between 11 and 15 "B" answers** indicates that your habitual reaction to stress is low. You have what is known as a "Type B" stress style. Like extreme Type As, extreme Type Bs are uncommon. But if this is your style, you are laid back, mellow, and tolerant. You philosophically take setbacks in stride, always mindful of the fact that "This, too, shall pass."

◆ **A total of between 8 and 10 "B" answers** indicates that your habitual reaction to stress is moderately low. You are a moderate Type B. For the most part you keep your cool. Even though you may blow your stack once in a while, you are fairly patient and relaxed. You are often willing to let events unfold before jumping in and deciding to "do something." You are probably perceived as fairly gentle and accepting of others.

Note: In neutral situations, Type As and Type Bs can appear to be pretty much the same, but their behaviors alter rapidly as the stakes in any given situation escalate. Tell a group of Type As they're about to be tested on a difficult task and given electric shocks for incorrect answers, for example, and their pulse rate and blood pressure rise much more rapidly than do those of Type Bs.

7

How Assertive Am I?

Are you assertive? You might hasten to say, "Oh no, I'm a nice person." But the two traits are not mutually exclusive. You don't have to be hostile, abrasive, or bossy to be assertive. You just need to be able to set boundaries, to ask appropriately for what you need, and to say "no" when that is warranted.

A certain amount of assertiveness is essential if you are going to be effective in managing your commitments, maintaining control of your life, and managing stress. Have you got it? Take the following quiz and find out.

Take the Test

This test has two sections to it. First, for each of the following statements, indicate the number of the statement that corresponds to your level of agreement or disagreement:

1. Strongly disagree

2. Somewhat disagree

3. Feel neutral or are not sure

4. Somewhat agree

5. Strongly agree

When you complete this part, follow the directions for the next section, which will involve responding to some hypothetical scenarios:

1. I don't mind asking a friend for a favor.

2. I strongly influence how my friends and I spend leisure time.

3. I'd be mortified if someone called me "pushy."

4. I will ask for a raise if I feel I deserve it.

5. I take the lead in planning family vacations.

6. I will speak up if someone cuts in line ahead of me.

7. I know how to set limits with my kids.

8. I have trouble saying "no" to whatever my boss asks of me.

9. I would point out to my spouse or romantic partner if she hurt my feelings.

10. I'll do anything to avoid a confrontation.

11. I can resist high-pressure sales pitches.

12. I relish a good political argument.

13. I'll say "no" to my parents if they make unreasonable requests.

14. If I am getting poor customer service, I will ask for a supervisor.

15. I would send back restaurant food that was not what I ordered.

16. I would decline to do others' work without credit or compensation.

17. I tend to say "sorry" when I feel I haven't really done anything wrong.

18. I'm not intimidated by attractive members of the opposite sex.

19. I get embarrassed by compliments.

20. I will offer constructive criticism when warranted.

21. If I buy defective merchandise, I will return it.

22. I generally just go along to get along.

23. I pretend to agree with views I do not hold, just to keep the peace.

24. I get quiet around people who are loud.

25. People say I am funny or witty.

26. I give praise and compliments when they are deserved.

27. I've been the first to say "I love you" in a relationship.

28. If my spouse/partner agrees to do something and does not, I remind him.

29. If someone interrupts me when I'm speaking, I'll just stop.

30. I'll stick up for myself if unjustly criticized.

31. I could decline a request to lend money to a friend.

32. I am nervous around authority figures.

33. I would question a teacher or other expert who I thought was wrong.

34. I'll point out if someone's teasing is making me uncomfortable.

35. If an unfair policy were implemented at work, I would speak up.

36. If I see a more efficient way to do something at work, I will point it out.

37. I'd point out a mistake on a restaurant or hotel bill.

38. I only feel comfortable complaining in writing.

39. If a co-worker blames me for something I did not do, I will defend myself.

40. I'm thought of as opinionated.

Now, for the following five scenarios, indicate whether you would be most likely to respond to the situation with the behavior in option A, B, or C. Choose the action that most closely matches what you would do and say:

1. You're about to take off on a cross-country flight. Someone asks you to switch seats with him so he can sit across the aisle from his spouse. This would put you in a middle seat for five hours, which you specifically tried to avoid by booking early. You ...

   A. Agree to switch, even though you deeply resent the inconvenience.

   B. Politely decline, without overly explaining yourself or apologizing.

   C. Refuse, saying, "You have some nerve. You should have thought about seating assignments ahead of time."

2. A co-worker whom you know makes less money than you do asks you if she can borrow $20. She borrowed $20 from you almost a month ago and has never paid you back, and never mentioned that loan. You ...

   A. Sigh and cough up the cash, rationalizing that you can't refuse if you make more money than she does.

   B. Calmly explain that you will be unable to make her another loan.

   C. Say, "You've got to be kidding! Where's the money I already lent you? Did you conveniently 'forget'?"

3. Your dentist's receptionist calls and asks if you would mind coming in an hour later than planned for your appointment. This puts you at risk for being late to an important meeting later in the day. You …

   A. Agree, hoping your whole day doesn't go awry, because—after all—your dentist is a busy professional.

   B. You say you have a conflict, and reschedule for another day.

   C. Insist that the dentist see you on time, as planned, or lose you as a patient.

4. You are completing the purchase of a new HDTV. The salesperson is aggressively pushing what you consider to be a very expensive and unnecessary service plan. You are running short on time and just want to conclude the transaction and get your TV home. You …

   A. Sign up for the plan.

   B. Firmly decline the plan and ask for a manager if the salesperson persists.

   C. Say, "I told you I don't want your #@%* plan," and storm out without completing the purchase.

5. You are sitting in a restaurant that has a no-smoking policy when someone lights up a cigar. You are very sensitive to smoke. You …

   A. Hope someone says something.

   B. Ask the server or restaurant manager to say something to the offender.

   C. Walk over and stub out his cigar yourself.

Scoring and Explanation

To obtain the first part of your score, tally your points. But before doing so, be sure to *reverse the score (5 = 1, 4 = 2, 3 = 3, 2 = 4, 1 = 5) for the following items:* 3, 8, 10, 17, 19, 22, 23, 24, 29, 32, 38. Remember, in reversing the score, high numbers are traded for low and vice versa.

Unless you reverse the scores for the items listed—and *only* for the items listed—your result will be inaccurate. See the Introduction to this book for a full explanation of reverse scoring.

To obtain the second part of your score, give yourself 5 points for each "B" response, but no points for "A" or "C" responses.

Add the two parts of your score together to get your final result:

◆ **A score of 175–225** indicates that you have a high degree of assertiveness. You are anything but a shrinking violet. You know what you need, have a strong sense of what is fair and unfair, and speak out accordingly. In most instances, this can serve you well. But if you are on the high end of the scale (over 200), do consider that it is also wise to pick your battles. You might not need to right *every* wrong with such gusto.

 I encourage very high scorers to take a special look at your responses to the five scenarios in Part 2 of this assessment. If you answered "C" to more than one question (we'll overlook a one-time press of a special "hot button"), you may well be crossing the line from assertiveness to aggression too often. The latter type of behavior can be self-destructive. It goes beyond the socially appropriate expression of feelings to belligerent words and actions that may provoke equally intense—and possibly escalating—responses. Studies also show that aggressive people are at greater risk for stress-related illnesses such as hypertension and heart disease. A simple strategy such as breathing deeply before you respond to a provocation can be a start to changing what has become a habitual overreaction to frustration.

◆ **A score of 130–174** indicates that you are moderately assertive. You are willing to stand up for yourself in some situations, but hold back in others. Notice where your lowest score responses lie and see whether you can identify a pattern. Perhaps you are less apt to speak up for yourself in work situations than you are in your relationship, or vice versa. If there is a particular circumstance in which you are continually being taken advantage of, see if you can gradually begin to articulate your needs in a way that can be heard and understood.

◆ **A score of 129 or below** suggests that you are reluctant to assert yourself. You could likely benefit from being more forceful and from saying "no" more often. The squeaky wheel gets the grease, and you are not squeaking. Create some rules for yourself ("I do not make loans to friends" or "I do not work on weekends") and practice saying those rules aloud.

Be advised that when you start to be more assertive, you will encounter resistance in others who have known you for some time. Certain that they can prevail, they will only step up their efforts to control you. You will need to stick to your new behavior (though it may feel uncomfortable and unfamiliar for some time) until they realize you are serious about change.

How Creative Am I?

Everyone's capable of creativity, especially during childhood. That's when we are all open to wonder and awe, and when the fun of experimentation is part of everyday life. But not all of us develop enduring creative habits or sustain innovative ways of thinking that last a lifetime.

If you wonder if you're as creative as you can be or as you might like to be, take this assessment and find out.

Take the Test

For each of the following statements, indicate the number of the statement that corresponds to your level of agreement or disagreement:

---

1. Strongly disagree

2. Somewhat disagree

3. Feel neutral or are not sure

4. Somewhat agree

5. Strongly agree

---

1. I tend to follow my hunches.

2. Some of my best ideas about a project pop up when I'm not actually working on it.

3. I have a childlike appreciation of new, silly, or playful things.

4. I think humankind has already made most of its great leaps.

5. Sometimes I solve problems in my dreams.

6. I am very flexible—if one approach doesn't work I'll just try another.

7. I don't see the point of working at something just for the fun of it.

8. In my mind, I have sometimes associated certain sounds or numbers with certain colors.

9. I have come up with unusual solutions to problems.

10. I see the world differently than others and want to share my worldview.

11. I am primarily motivated by money.

12. Often I just know things without knowing how I know them.

13. I sometimes find humor in things when most others don't.

14. I don't consider an idea to be creative unless it is useful.

15. Some people think of me as an oddball.

16. I enjoy puns and other wordplay.

17. I am primarily motivated by a desire for recognition.

18. Once I already have in mind the way I want to do something, I won't change the way I do it.

19. When I read a novel, I have vivid pictures of the characters and settings in my mind.

20. I am very concerned with other people's opinions of me.

21. I always have a Plan B.

22. I like to try new combinations of food, clothing, and other things.

23. I am comfortable with unconventional people.

24. I am uncomfortable breaking rules.

25. I think it is cheating to be inspired by someone else's work.

26. Even if something is good, it can always be better.

27. I have gotten up early or stayed up late to pursue an idea.

28. If someone laughs at me, that's her problem.

29. When I am working on something I like, I lose track of time.

30. Nothing is impossible.

Scoring and Explanation

Before tallying your total points, be sure to *reverse the score* (5 = 1, 4 = 2, 3 = 3, 2 = 4, 1 = 5) *for the following items:* 4, 7, 11, 14, 17, 18, 20, 24, 25. Remember, in reversing the score, high numbers are traded for low and vice versa. Unless you reverse the scores for the items listed— and *only* for the items listed—your result will be inaccurate. See the Introduction to this book for a full explanation of reverse scoring.

Tally your points:

◆ **A score of 125–150** indicates that you are highly creative. You are unconventional, unorthodox, and unlikely to do things a certain way just because that's the way they've always been done. You are internally motivated and eternally curious. You feel most alive when you are pursuing an idea that's gotten hold of you, and you won't be dissuaded when you're on a creative roll.

◆ **A score of 95–124** indicates that you have some definite creative tendencies, but you are not always comfortable marching to your own drummer. Perhaps if you gave a bit less credence to the judgments of traditional types, you'd have a true breakthrough.

◆ **A score of 94 or below** indicates that many of your creative abilities are currently latent. Remember, everybody has the potential for creativity, so if you'd like to up your score, consider dabbling in some new pastimes. Start by exposing yourself to the company of creative types, and allowing yourself to simply fantasize.

Part 2

My Personality at Work

Are you in the job that's right for you? Are you cut out to strike out on your own? Do you have what it takes to be not just a boss, but a great boss? In this section of the book, you uncover aspects of your personality that can give your career a boost. And you might target potentially troublesome traits in time to keep them from holding you back.

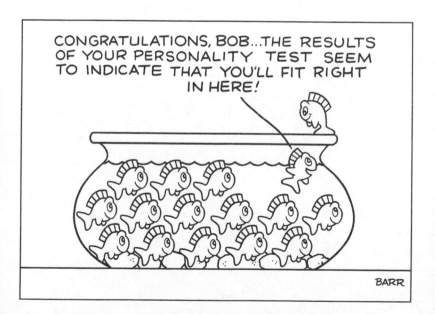

Would I Make a Great Boss?

If you've ever been disgruntled at work—and who hasn't?—you have probably entertained the thought that you would do a much better job of being in charge than the folks who currently *are* in charge. You could be right. Or, maybe not.

Being an effective boss is a challenging role. Take this assessment and see how you are likely to do if your dream of leadership becomes a reality.

Take the Test

For each of the following statements, indicate whether you think the statement is TRUE or FALSE:

1. A good boss should be considered a good friend by everyone who works for him.

2. An effective boss has to be a good communicator.

3. A boss should never change her mind once she makes a decision.

4. A boss should seek suggestions from employees about improving work processes.

5. An effective boss keeps a low profile.

6. Employees perform better if you provide opportunities to socialize and have fun at work.

7. Employees will automatically be happier if you just give them more money.

8. A boss should not hire subordinates who are more intelligent than he.

9. A boss need not worry about whether his employees have adequate time to spend with their families.

10. A boss should be involved in every little detail of her organization.

Scoring and Explanation

Give yourself one point for each of your answers that matches the following answer key. Brief explanations of the answers are provided:

1. FALSE. Employees often have mixed emotions toward their bosses. But a boss shouldn't spend his time worrying about being popular, or he will be afraid to make decisions that may be unpopular but are still sound.

2. TRUE. Some bad bosses hoard information on purpose, because they think this gives them more power. Some bad bosses don't share information because they are just not effective speakers or

writers. Either way, when employees don't know what's going on, they don't know *why* they are doing what they're doing. Their lack of purpose translates into lethargy.

3. FALSE. Changing your mind as shifting circumstances warrant, or when evidence indicates your initial plan was misguided, is a hallmark of flexibility and pragmatism. Both are desirable qualities in a leader.

4. TRUE. Employees are more satisfied and perform better when they participate in decisions regarding their work. Besides, no one knows better than the people on the front lines how their job should be done.

5. FALSE. To be effective, a boss must not only have a vision, but also be *visible* as she works to make that vision come true.

6. TRUE. Job performance goes up when people feel bonded to those they work with. Sharing good times builds team spirit.

7. FALSE. Job satisfaction does not depend on compensation (so long as compensation is fair) so much as it does on feeling that one is in a job where he is using his talents and achieving a meaningful goal.

8. TRUE. A good boss does not let his ego get in the way of hiring the best and the brightest.

9. FALSE. Employee performance and retention improves when workers are enabled to lead a more flexible balance of work and life.

10. FALSE. Being an effective leader is not about micromanaging. A good boss stays focused on the big picture, and leaves the workday details to trusted others on the front lines.

◆ **If you matched 9–10 answers,** you would be a very effective boss. You have the right priorities and a keen understanding of what people look for in a leader. Do all you can do to get your organization to recognize your potential—or look for an organization that will!

◆ **If you matched 7–8 answers,** you are almost—but not quite—ready to assume a leadership role. Review the responses where your answers diverged from the answer key, and make an effort to be more observant of workplace dynamics. Also, think about what you have learned from the bosses you've respected and admired.

◆ **If you matched 6 or fewer answers,** that suggests you're not ready to be the boss yet. However, true leaders are made—not born. It would be a good idea for you to read some books and articles that contain the latest research on leadership, management skills, and employee satisfaction.

Am I a Team Player?

Teamwork! You might remember the word from your days playing soccer in middle school or rowing on college crew. But chances are, you are also hearing it in the workplace. Many organizations pride themselves on the successes of their teams and their commitment to the team ethic. Although the trend toward working in teams was initiated several decades ago, it has proved to have staying power, because high-functioning teams have continually produced credible innovations.

But for a team to *be* high functioning—i.e., for the whole to be greater than the sum of its parts—it must consist of members who possess the skills that teamwork demands. Are you a team player, or would you really rather go it alone?

Take the Test

For each of the following statements, indicate the letter of the statement with which you agree:

1. When you are asked to participate in a team effort at work, you …

    A. Do everything you can to avoid the assignment.

    B. Look forward to the process.

    C. Immediately try to figure out how to get to be team leader.

2. When you are asked to share information with team members, you …

    A. Share everything you know.

    B. Hold something back—knowledge is power.

    C. Fear that someone will challenge you.

3. What is your opinion on brainstorming sessions?

    A. They're a waste of time.

    B. They get my juices flowing.

    C. I can never seem to get a word in.

4. Who do you believe is more likely to come up with a good solution to a problem?

    A. A group working together.

    B. A group under clear direction.

    C. A smart individual.

5. If your team was failing to reach consensus because of one stubborn individual, you would …

    A. Eject or ignore that individual.

    B. Allow her to air her objections, and then vote.

    C. I *am* that individual.

6. In general, how likely are you to change your opinion when compelling new information is introduced?

    A. Highly unlikely.

    B. Not very likely.

    C. Very likely.

7. In general, how flexible are you when it comes to trying new methods and techniques for solving a problem?

    A. Highly flexible.

    B. Not very flexible.

    C. Inflexible.

8. In general, what time frame do you employ for solving problems?

    A. I like to mull my options over and "sleep on it" if possible.

    B. I like to jump on it immediately.

    C. I like to stall and hope it will go away.

9. In general, how would you rate your ability to listen?

    A. I am usually planning what I'll say next, rather than listening.

    B. I am a careful listener.

    C. What'd you say?

10. In general, how do you think fellow team members would describe you?

    A. Keeps a low profile.

    B. Cooperative, collaborative, creative.

    C. A royal pain.

Scoring and Explanation

Give yourself one point for each of your answers that matches the following answer key:

1. B	6. C
2. A	7. A
3. B	8. A
4. A	9. B
5. B	10. B

◆ **A score of 9–10** indicates that you are a valuable team member. You would probably also make a good team facilitator. You have the requisite skill set—including flexibility, patience, and communication savvy. Just as important (perhaps most important of all), you are a true believer in the power of teams. You'd likely agree with anthropologist Margaret Mead, who said, "Never doubt that a small group of thoughtful, committed people can change the world. Indeed, it is the only thing that ever has."

◆ **A score of 7–8** indicates that you have a moderate level of teamwork skills. Notice where your areas of divergence are. Are you perhaps a little impatient? A tad rigid in your opinions? If you relax a bit and trust the team process, you can make more valuable contributions and actually enjoy working in teams more than you do today.

◆ **A score of 6 or below** suggests that you are not comfortable working in a team setting. Perhaps you do work best as a solo act, but it wouldn't hurt to expand your repertoire in the workplace. You just might discover some new sides of yourself and expand on the magnitude of what you can accomplish.

What's My "Office Politics" IQ?

Relationships matter in the workplace. Whether we like it or not, our people smarts, diplomatic skills, discretion, and instincts for self-preservation all play a role in our level of success. Indeed, we can probably all think of people who wound up on the fast track—or the unemployment line—due to their high (or low) degree of political office savvy.

What's your level of emotional sophistication when it comes to office politics?

Take the Test

For each of the following statements, indicate the letter of the statement you agree with:

1. When it comes to your boss, you believe your role is …

    A. To make her look good.

    B. To prove you know more than she does.

    C. To stay out of her way.

2. When it comes time to volunteer for a challenging assignment, you …

    A. Step up if it is something you can handle.

    B. Are sure you will get it, even if you're not sure how to do it.

    C. Hide in the restroom.

3. When it comes time for your performance review, you …

    A. Are reluctant to blow your own horn.

    B. Make sure you are well prepared to detail your accomplishments.

    C. Are still hiding in the restroom.

4. If you get a call from a headhunter, you …

    A. Brag to your colleagues.

    B. Are very discreet, even if you are interested.

    C. Rush off to make copies of your resumé on the office copying machine.

5. If a co-worker tries to take credit for your accomplishments, you …

    A. Immediately call him out in front of everyone.

    B. Diplomatically make sure your boss knows about your contributions.

    C. Just grin and bear it.

6. If you see a co-worker being rewarded by your boss, even though her work is subpar, you ...

   A. Confront your boss and point out this person's ineptitude.

   B. Tread carefully while trying to determine what your boss appreciates about her.

   C. Weep.

7. If a co-worker hints that he wants you to do something you think is unethical, you ...

   A. Ask, "What's in it for me?"

   B. Distance yourself from him and make it clear you believe his behavior is unacceptable.

   C. Immediately tattle.

8. A customer complains about you to your boss, and you think the complaint is unfair. You ...

   A. Explain to your boss why the customer is a jerk.

   B. Call the customer and chew her out.

   C. Assure your boss you will clear up any misunderstanding and repair the customer relationship.

9. If a co-worker is taking up too much of your time with chitchat, you ...

   A. Tell him to stop wasting your time.

   B. Ask your boss to tell him to stop wasting your time.

   C. Tell him you can't talk right now, then limit run-ins as best you can.

10. If someone you think of as a trusted mentor repeatedly gives you bad advice, you ...

    A. Distance yourself and stop taking his advice.

    B. Make excuses for him and keep following his lead.

    C. Publicly accuse him of sabotaging you.

11. If a supervisor is sexually harassing you, you …

    A. Assume you have no choice but to put up with it.

    B. Phone his spouse.

    C. Investigate appropriate complaint channels offered by Human Resources.

12. If a co-worker routinely hogs all the time in meetings, you …

    A. Make every effort to speak before she gets the floor.

    B. Roll your eyes, sigh, and loudly tap your fingers while she talks.

    C. Lie to her and tell her a meeting has been cancelled.

13. You know two co-workers are having an affair, but their relationship is not affecting their work or yours. You …

    A. Gleefully spread office gossip.

    B. Tell them to stop.

    C. Mind your own business.

14. A very competitive co-worker has lied to you, apparently to try to undermine you. You …

    A. Are careful to verify any information she gives you in the future.

    B. Automatically assume everything she says henceforth is a fabrication.

    C. Knowingly spread a false rumor about her.

15. You receive an inflammatory e-mail from your boss reprimanding you for something you did not do. You …

    A. Immediately fire back a defensive e-mail and copy the world.

    B. Request a personal meeting with your boss and explain your side of the issue.

    C. Barge into your boss's office and threaten to quit.

Scoring and Explanation

Give yourself one point for each of your answers that matches the following answer key:

1. A	6. B	11. C
2. A	7. B	12. A
3. B	8. C	13. C
4. B	9. C	14. A
5. B	10. A	15. B

◆ **A score of 13–15** indicates that you have a very high office politics IQ. The workplace is filled with emotional landmines, but you manage to sidestep them. You know when to speak up, when to lay low, and when to get more information before you act. Chances are you are on your way to an illustrious career.

◆ **A score of 10–12** indicates that you have a moderately high office politics IQ. Try to be a little less impulsive in your reactions, as this will lead to a higher level of self-protection. There are times when circumstances are unfair, but don't be unfair to yourself by making bad situations worse.

◆ **A score of 9 or below** suggests that your office politics IQ needs some work—lest you find yourself out of work. You need to take a deep breath—or preferably many deep breaths—before you react to a situation. The more angry or frustrated you feel, the longer you need to wait before embarking on a course of action. Don't let your emotions rule you. Remind yourself that it is within your power to rule them.

Quiz 12

Am I in the Right Job?

For better or worse, most of us spend far more time working than we do with our loved ones or enjoying our hobbies—or even sleeping! If we're in a job we find fulfilling, our daily life tends to be pretty satisfying. But if we are just marking time and getting a paycheck, or—worse—spending our workday feeling dejected or apathetic, a case can be made that we are frittering our life away.

Chances are, you already have a strong sense of whether or not you're in the right job. Take this quiz to see if your instincts are borne out.

Take the Test

For each of the following statements, indicate the number of the statement that corresponds to your level of agreement or disagreement:

1. Strongly disagree

2. Somewhat disagree

3. Feel neutral or are not sure

4. Somewhat agree

5. Strongly agree

1. I spend at least part of my workday using my particular strengths and talents.

2. I have input in decisions that affect my daily work.

3. I have good friends among the people I work with.

4. I understand the purpose behind what I am doing.

5. At work, I often daydream.

6. I take pride in excelling in my work.

7. If I won a lottery jackpot tomorrow, I'd still keep my job.

8. I am distrustful of the people I work for.

9. Time flies during the course of my workday.

10. I feel appreciated for my efforts.

11. I'd encourage young people to do what I do.

12. I have fun at work.

13. I know exactly how much vacation and sick time I have coming.

14. I'd be disappointed if my kids followed in my footsteps.

15. No one ever thanks me for the work I do.

16. I feel respected by those I work with and for.

17. I am a clock-watcher.

18. I laugh several times a day at work.

19. If I have an idea about improving something, someone will listen to me.

20. I often fantasize about early retirement.

Scoring and Explanation

Before tallying your total points, be sure to *reverse the score* (5 = 1, 4 = 2, 3 = 3, 2 = 4, 1 = 5) *for the following items:* 5, 8, 13, 14, 15, 17, 20. Remember, in reversing the score, high numbers are traded for low and vice versa. Unless you reverse the scores for the items listed—and *only* for the items listed—your result will be inaccurate. See the Introduction to this book for a full explanation of reverse scoring.

Tally your points:

◆ **A score of 80–100** indicates that you are certainly in the right job. You enjoy your work. You take pride in what you do and feel appreciated for the role you play in the big picture. Your positive feelings about work probably mean that you have a good self-image and a high degree of overall life happiness.

◆ **A score of 68–79** indicates that you are in a job that has many positives for you, but also some negatives. Notice which of your responses yielded low numbers. Are you feeling that your talents are underutilized? Are you not being given enough of a participatory role? If there are things you can do to improve your situation, think about proactive measures. If you feel there is no hope of improvement, you might start to explore other options.

◆ **A score of 67 or below** indicates that you are not in a job you enjoy. You do not feel that your abilities are being used, or that you are acknowledged for what you do. You might have good reasons for staying in this job, such as immediate financial security. If that's the case, don't do anything rash. On the other hand, if you stay in a job you consider a dead-end for too long, you could suffer burnout, depression, and other emotional downsides. So do try to come up with a long-term plan. Seek career counseling, if you could use some professional input. Consider getting some additional education that can increase your options. Meanwhile, network like crazy. You never know who's got the inside line on a job that's right up your alley.

13

Should I Be Self-Employed?

Do you have the entrepreneurial itch? And if so, is it really time to scratch it?

Many people dream of leaving their employee days behind and making a go of it on their own—whether it's to freelance or to build an empire. There's no doubt that being self-employed has its rewards. You get to be the decision-maker. And your boss won't torment you. But if you're not disciplined in numerous ways, you might find yourself unemployed rather than self-employed. The following quiz will help you decide if you've got the right stuff to go solo.

Take the Test

For each of the following statements, indicate the number of the statement that corresponds to your level of agreement or disagreement:

1. Strongly disagree

2. Somewhat disagree

3. Feel neutral or are not sure

4. Somewhat agree

5. Strongly agree

1. I am self-motivated.

2. I love to talk about my work.

3. I persist even when the odds are against me.

4. I am very clear about my values and beliefs.

5. I genuinely enjoy my work.

6. I am a pessimist.

7. I am an "ideas person" who leaves details to others.

8. I am reluctant to remind people when they owe me money.

9. I resent having to work on weekends.

10. I am willing to sacrifice short-term pleasures for long-term goals.

11. I have a clear vision of where I want to be five years from now.

12. I am well organized.

13. I like to network with people in my field.

14. I keep up with developments in my field.

15. I am impatient with difficult clients.

16. I take pride in what I do.

17. I procrastinate on tasks I dislike.

18. I am deeply bonded with friends at my current job.

19. I am a good communicator.

20. I like to think of ways to improve upon what I do.

Scoring and Explanation

Before tallying your total points, be sure to *reverse the score* (5 = 1, 4 = 2, 3 = 3, 2 = 4, 1 = 5) *for the following items:* 6, 7, 8, 9, 15, 17, 18. Remember, in reversing the score, high numbers are traded for low and vice versa. Unless you reverse the scores for the items listed—and *only* for the items listed—your result will be inaccurate. See the Introduction to this book for a full explanation of reverse scoring.

Tally your points:

◆ **A score of 81–100** suggests a high chance of self-employment success. You are self-motivated and self-disciplined. Most important of all, you love what you do, and you do what you love. All of this points to your potential as a self-starter.

◆ **A score of 70–80** indicates that you are on the fence. It's not clear that it's yet time to jump to the other side. While you have some traits and attitudes that bode well for your taking charge of your professional fate, there is also some evidence that you'd be more content remaining in someone else's employ.

◆ **A score of 69 or below** suggests you would *not* be comfortable out there on your own. Don't worry; self-employment is not for everyone. There's no stigma at all in working as part of an organization managed by others. Chances are you'll be satisfied, so long as you're doing something you find meaningful and rewarding.

Quiz **14**

Am I a Good Interview?

No matter how strong your resumé is and how much experience you have, the impression you make during a job interview is the crucial factor in whether or not you will actually land the position you want. Interviewing successfully requires a particular set of skills comprised of one part social intelligence, one part emotional prescience, one part conversational finesse, and one part grooming and fashion sense.

Have you got what it takes to turn an interview into an opportunity—or are you more likely to be back pounding the pavement after your face-to-face encounter? Take this assessment and see.

And by the way, if you don't think there's a job interview in your near future, think again. The average worker under 35 interviews once every 18 months, and the average worker over 35 interviews once every 3 years.

Take the Test

For each of the following statements, indicate the letter of the statement you agree with:

1. How much research are you likely to do on a prospective employer before the interview?

    A. I google them.

    B. I do Internet research and more, such as trying to find someone with direct knowledge of the company.

    C. I do little or none: I figure they'll tell me what I need to know.

2. You think it is most important to make a strong impression …

    A. In the first two minutes of the interview.

    B. In the first ten minutes of the interview.

    C. As the interview is concluding.

3. If asked why this company should hire you, you …

    A. Use adjectives to describe your good attributes.

    B. Try to be humble.

    C. Talk about concrete things you've accomplished.

4. If asked if you have any questions, you …

    A. Assure the interviewer you have none.

    B. Are ready with a long list of questions on every aspect of the company.

    C. Ask one or two very specific questions about the position.

5. If you are asked if you have any shortcomings, you …

    A. Assure the interviewer you have none.

    B. Mention an area you're currently working on to enhance your performance.

    C. Are sure to honestly list everything that might be considered a flaw.

6. When you dress for an interview, you …

   A. Dress casually so they won't think you're too eager.

   B. Dress in very expensive designer clothing.

   C. Dress like a well-dressed employee at that particular company.

7. With regard to your overall appearance, you try to look …

   A. Uniquely fashionable and memorable.

   B. Buttoned down and conservative.

   C. Like you belong.

8. If you are asked why you left a previous job—and the truth is you were fired, you …

   A. Say you quit.

   B. Calmly and briefly tell the truth from your perspective.

   C. Explain why your last boss was a jerk.

9. When interacting with the interviewer, you try to …

   A. Smile and make eye contact.

   B. Consciously mirror every move he makes.

   C. Ask him personal questions about his family.

10. When the interview is over, you …

    A. Ask if you got the job.

    B. Send a thank-you along with any follow-up information that's appropriate.

    C. Pray.

Scoring and Explanation

Give yourself one point for each of your answers that matches the following answer key:

1. B. You should be as informed as possible. You want to be perceived as someone who does his homework. Besides, knowledge will always give you an edge.

2. A. Like it or not, initial impressions are the most important. In fact, research shows that hiring decisions are often clinched on a subconscious level within the first few *seconds* of an interview. Equally important, it is almost impossible to recover if you fumble at the start.

3. C. It's best to make your points with anecdotes, not adjectives. The former is evidence; the latter can come off as empty grandiosity.

4. C. Asking nothing makes you look uninterested; asking things you could have easily found out beforehand makes you look un-prepared. Asking good questions is a sign of a sharp mind.

5. B. Hey, nobody's perfect! It's arrogant to pretend to be so. But on the other hand, you don't want to enumerate your every foible. Highlight an area where you are somewhat strong but plan to be even stronger, and tell how you are working on strengthening your skill.

6. C. Find out the standard of dress for employees in the type of position you desire. Your apparel should be appropriate within the context of your targeted organization's culture.

7. C. Once again, you want to look like you fit in with the specific culture where you are interviewing. It's okay to be fashion-forward if you are interviewing for, say, a job at a fashion magazine. And it's okay to look buttoned down if you are interviewing at a private banking firm. But think how self-destructive it would be to do the reverse!

8. B. Dishonesty is never a good policy (and do remember how easy it could be for a prospective employer to check your version of events). Neither is it a good idea to use an interview to air your

grievances. Keep your explanation straight and simple, and move on. Almost everyone's been fired at one time or another.

9. A. Smiling and making eye contact goes toward making that all-important positive first impression. As for mirroring the interviewer's movements, you may have heard that this is a surefire path to success—but when it is done too overtly (as it often is), it can be downright creepy. Also creepy and inappropriate is asking about an interviewer's private life.

10. B. Not to belittle the power of prayer, but even if you engage in it, it wouldn't hurt to follow up with a courteous thank-you and some additional information.

Tally your total number of matching responses:

◆ **A score of 9 or 10** indicates that you are ready to interview. You are willing to do the proper preparation, and you know how to conduct yourself in an appropriate way. Good luck in your new job!

◆ **A score of 7 or 8** indicates that your interview skills could stand a little brushing up. Notice the answers where your responses diverged and be sure that you are at the top of your game before you go forth and interview. Remember, an interview is not a dress rehearsal. There rarely are "do-overs," and hiring decisions are made quickly.

◆ **A score of 6 or below** suggests that you are not yet ready for a face-to-face encounter. In addition to reviewing the information here, do some additional research on honing your interview skills. Then consider asking someone to help you rehearse. Have her play the role of interviewer and run through possible questions and scenarios.

15

Am I a Strong Speaker?

With business competition fierce, and with so many ideas and technologies competing for attention, today it's more important than ever to have speaking skills in the workplace—and everywhere you may be networking. This assessment is designed to find out how well you perform in speaking situations. But it is also constructed to test your knowledge of certain essential communication dynamics. Your score will represent how much you know about communicating with an audience and how well you put what you know into practice.

Take the Test

Indicate whether you think each statement is TRUE or FALSE:

1. I always prepare and rehearse before a presentation.

2. After hearing my presentation, people can distill its main message into one sentence.

3. I feel a bit of nervous energy before a presentation.

4. Typically, people forget 40 percent of what they hear by the end of a presentation.

5. I try to anticipate difficult questions audience members might ask.

6. I am always terrified someone will ask me a question I can't answer.

7. Audience interest is always highest at the start of a speech or presentation.

8. I am always looking to add new information to a standard presentation.

9. I never rephrase what I say or how I say it, no matter who my audience is.

10. I pay a lot of attention to choosing just the right opening words.

11. If I lose my place I get very flustered.

12. I always start a presentation with a popular joke I've memorized.

13. Using visual images can increase audience retention.

14. I always support what I say with evidence like facts, figures, and examples.

15. There's no such thing as putting too much information in a presentation.

16. People remember anecdotes more than any other type of material.

17. Lincoln's Gettysburg Address was 10 sentences long.

18. I prepare a presentation based strictly on what slides I already have.

19. I put as much information as possible on each slide.

20. Interactive techniques like polling the audience increase audience attention.

21. I rarely move around or gesture when I am speaking.

22. I like to use analogies and comparisons in my talks.

23. I avoid smiling during presentations because it makes me seem less credible.

24. I always have a backup plan should my slide projector or other technology fail.

25. I would feel comfortable claiming my share of time on a panel discussion.

Scoring and Explanation

Give yourself one point for each of your answers that matches the following answer key:

1. TRUE. Practice is a must.

2. TRUE. People should come away knowing your headline.

3. TRUE. A little nervous energy keeps you vibrant.

4. TRUE. This is all too true, so repeat what's important in various ways.

5. TRUE. You can't be too prepared.

6. FALSE. Good speakers have answers to tough questions at the ready.

7. TRUE. Make your strongest points early.

8. TRUE. Good speakers keep their material fresh.

9. FALSE. You'll get stale if you don't change things up.

10. TRUE. The opening is the most critical part.

11. FALSE. No reason to panic—the audience is not your enemy.

12. FALSE. Humor can be effective, but memorized jokes tend to fall flat.

13. TRUE. People have a higher retention when words are paired with images.

14. TRUE. Proving your points makes you credible.

15. FALSE. People blank out if you overload information.

16. TRUE. Everyone loves a good story.

17. TRUE. Lincoln was a master of brevity and depth.

18. FALSE. Create slides to support messages you want to share.

19. FALSE. Crowded slides distract from you and confuse the audience.

20. TRUE. It pays to get everyone involved.

21. FALSE. It's boring to be a statue.

22. TRUE. Analogies give people examples that make sense in everyday life.

23. FALSE. Unless your news is dire, smiling helps you convey any message.

24. TRUE. Stuff happens—be ready!

25. TRUE. Panel discussions are no time to be shy.

◆ **A score of 20–25** indicates that you are an exceptionally strong speaker. You have an implicit understanding of how people really *listen*. You also have good habits and sound instincts about what to do in front of an audience. Chances are high that your speaking style and penchant for clear communication will help you get ahead.

◆ **A score of 13–19** indicates that you have some very strong points as a speaker, but could improve some aspects of your skill set. Take a look at where your responses diverged from the answer key to get an idea of what you might learn more about. There are many good books on presentation skills that can help you on your way. Or you can join a group like Toastmasters.

◆ **A score of 12 or below** indicates that public speaking is probably not your strong suit. Don't worry; you're hardly alone. As comedian Jerry Seinfeld once commented, many people would be more comfortable being a corpse than giving a eulogy. But speaking skills are increasingly important in the workplace; in most occupations it won't do to duck under your desk every time information needs to be conveyed or a pitch needs to be made. If you've taken this quiz, it is probably because you already have an interest in improving your skills, so set a course of action and stick to it. Books, DVDs, and workshops on public speaking abound. If you work for a large company your employer may already have a speaking coach on hand to train employees. Please note: if you took Quiz 1 in this book and determined that you are an introvert, that's still no excuse. The point of training is to be armed with tools and techniques that will help you gain confidence in public situations.

How Conscientious Am I?

Conscientiousness refers to the inclination to work hard, to be thorough, and to be dependable and responsible. It also tends to relate to one's ability to subscribe to socially prescribed expectations. Conscientiousness—or lack thereof—is considered to be a major personality trait.

Conscientiousness is a particularly interesting personality trait because it can continue to develop well into adulthood. (So, even if you were a major slacker as an adolescent, you could be conscientious today.) Perhaps this is because society tends to offer many rewards to those who are industrious.

Not too surprising, conscientiousness correlates with high job-performance ratings and professional achievement. But what you may not know is that it also tends to correlate with healthy lifestyle behaviors, longevity, and even with marital stability.

Are you conscientious? Here's a chance to find out.

Take the Test

For each of the following statements, indicate the number of the statement that corresponds to your level of agreement or disagreement:

1. Strongly disagree

2. Somewhat disagree

3. Feel neutral or are not sure

4. Somewhat agree

5. Strongly agree

1. I only make promises I know I can keep.

2. I will work as hard as necessary to meet a deadline.

3. I take personal pride in my work.

4. I won't shortcut a task if it means lessening the quality of my work.

5. I'm not especially punctual.

6. I know where I can find everything I need to get a job done.

7. People see me as someone they can count on.

8. I enjoy researching to find the best solution to a problem.

9. I am very fastidious about personal health and hygiene.

10. I vacillate when making decisions.

11. I get very wrapped up in my work.

12. I am concerned with following appropriate social protocols.

13. I have a lot of self-control.

14. I am good at following directions.

15. I procrastinate on parts of a task or job I do not like to do.

16. I use willpower to resist temptation.

17. I tend to get more diligent and determined as I grow older.

18. I know how to conduct myself in virtually any social situation.

19. I am spontaneous, and I dislike making plans.

20. If I were to visit a foreign country on business, I would research its culture first.

21. I look to find out what the speed limit is wherever I am driving.

22. If I am taking medication, I take it on schedule and as prescribed.

23. I tend to observe family or religious traditions.

24. I'm good about remembering birthdays and anniversaries.

25. I am accident-prone.

Scoring and Explanation

Before tallying your total points, be sure to *reverse the score* (5 = 1, 4 = 2, 3 = 3, 2 = 4, 1 = 5) *for the following items:* 5, 10, 15, 19, 25. Remember, in reversing the score, high numbers are traded for low and vice versa. Unless you reverse the scores for the items listed—and *only* for the items listed—your result will be inaccurate. See the Introduction to this book for a full explanation of reverse scoring.

Tally your points:

◆ **A score of 101–125** indicates a high level of conscientiousness. You are focused and goal-directed. You have good impulse control and are willing to delay short-term gratification if it gets in the way of what you wish to accomplish in the long run. You are scrupulous about making a game plan and carrying through with that plan. Chances are you start each day with a to-do list and don't quit until you have checked each item off. Those whom you live and work with know they can count on you.

◆ **A score of 81–100** indicates a moderate level of conscientiousness. You can do a pretty good job of accomplishing what you want when you have a mind to, but there are circumstances in which you'll cheerfully cut a few corners. You may have some resistance to following rules prescribed by others, and you'll look for loopholes now and then.

◆ **A score of 80 or below** suggests a relatively low level of conscientiousness. Chances are you can easily be distracted from achieving a goal if a pleasurable temptation beckons. But at the end of the day, you may wonder why it feels like you got few things done that you meant to get done. If you'd like to be more conscientious, there is certainly hope for you. This is a trait you can consciously work on, one step at a time. Try setting relatively modest goals that you know you can reach, and work toward them. As you achieve each one, your self-confidence will build and you can set a slightly grander goal. The key for you may lie in simple organizational techniques. Consider purchasing a day planner that will help you define your goals and help you keep track of how you spend your time.

17

Can I Handle Success?

"Fear of success" might sound like a contradiction in terms, but many people are conflicted about whether or not they can handle the acclaim, power, wealth, or notoriety that may accompany notable achievement. The reasons are many. Some feel undeserving. Some fear alienating those who are less successful. Some associate success with unpleasant trade-offs. Ironically, some people are afraid of success because they are afraid of failure. They are not willing to go all out in pursuit of their dreams, lest their hopes not be realized.

Unlike some personality constructs, most people who have fear of success are not consciously aware of having it. While someone might use "I'm shy" or "I'm conservative" as a descriptor, few are likely to label themselves as success-avoidant. The following test is designed to determine if you are, in fact, averse to success.

Take the Test

For each of the following statements, indicate the number of the statement that corresponds to your level of agreement or disagreement:

1. Strongly disagree

2. Somewhat disagree

3. Feel neutral or are not sure

4. Somewhat agree

5. Strongly agree

1. I don't enjoy being the center of attention.

2. I feel uncomfortable when I receive a compliment.

3. The successes I've had have been mostly due to luck.

4. I am perfectly capable of blowing my own horn.

5. I sometimes feel like an imposter.

6. I worry how people will judge me if I make a mistake.

7. I hate the idea that others might envy me.

8. I fear that those who envy me might wish me bad luck.

9. I am not very competitive.

10. Rewards have come too easily to me.

11. I believe I have had unfair advantages over others.

12. I've worked hard for everything I've achieved.

13. I would feel guilty if I became enormously wealthy.

14. I fear that I could lose all I have at any moment.

15. No matter what I accomplish, I feel I could have done better.

16. I have deliberately allowed others to beat me in games or at sports.

17. I hate the idea that anyone might resent me.

18. If I were wealthy and successful I would be able to do a lot of good for others.

19. I dislike it when people look to me for solutions to problems.

20. I am overqualified for my job.

21. I fear that my parents expected bigger things for me.

22. I am always setting new and higher goals.

23. I am fearful of being ridiculed.

24. I try not to set my sights too high for fear of being disappointed.

25. I'm not sure I know what my true purpose in life is.

26. I would hate to be called a show-off.

27. I have tried to play down my intelligence or expertise.

28. I love being proved right.

29. I go out of my way to make others look good, sometimes at my own expense.

30. I worry about being labeled pushy or assertive.

31. If I had to sacrifice certain friendships to be successful, I would.

32. I worry about how my life would change with major success.

33. Only shallow people care about worldly success.

34. Successful people inevitably become stuck-up.

35. Successful people inevitably become isolated.

36. Successful people are rarely liked for themselves.

37. It would surprise most people to know how competent and knowledgeable I am.

38. I deserve to be successful.

39. When you are successful, people always try to take advantage of you.

40. If I had to pick one, I would rather be remembered as a nice and humble person than as a success.

Scoring and Explanation

Before tallying your total points, be sure to *reverse the score* (5 = 1, 4 = 2, 3 = 3, 2 = 4, 1 = 5) *for the following items:* 4, 12, 18, 22, 28, 31, 38. Remember, in reversing the score, high numbers are traded for low and vice versa. Unless you reverse the scores for the items listed—and *only* for the items listed—your result will be inaccurate. See the Introduction to this book for a full explanation of reverse scoring.

Tally your points:

◆ **A score of 171–200** indicates that you are success-avoidant. On an emotional level, perhaps below your everyday level of awareness, you are resistant to achieving all that you can. On the plus side: now that you know this on a conscious level, you can take a look at how your fear might be taking its toll.

Are you unwittingly sabotaging yourself by undue modesty or by procrastination or other self-defeating behaviors? This self-sabotage and your fear probably go hand in glove. Often just becoming aware of a fear can be the beginning to getting it under control. It is easier to stop acting out on a fear once you can examine it in the light of day.

◆ **A score of 140–170** indicates that you are moderately success-avoidant. If you are just beginning your career, this is something you might simply grow out of in time as you become more secure in yourself. However, if you are further along, try looking at how your fears might be holding you back from fulfilling your potential. Write down your fears and take a hard look at them. Ask yourself: are they rational? If not, dispute them in your mind. Now, think of successful people who also seem happy and balanced. Let them be your role models.

◆ **A score of 139 or below** indicates that you are ready for success! Bring it on!

Part 3

My Personality in Love and Marriage

What are your strengths when it comes to relationships, and what are your shortcomings? No shortcomings, you say! Take the quizzes in this part of the book to find out just how thoughtful you are, how romantic you are, and whether or not you're a "clinger." You'll learn a few things about your sensuality and sexuality as well. Finally, you'll discover how likely it is that you're fated to happily live out your days with your mate.

EVEN BEFORE YOU TOOK THIS PERSONALITY TEST, I KNEW YOU WERE THE SWEETEST MAN I EVER MET!

BARR

How Romantic Am I?

Sure, you love your partner. But are you romantic? Do you display affection and voice your appreciation on a routine basis? Do you do sweet, endearing things that bring a smile to your lover's lips and make her heart go *pitter pat*? Saying you *used to* doesn't count. The following quiz will help you evaluate just how romantic you are in the here and now.

Take the Test

Count how many of the following statements apply to you. Give yourself one point for each applicable statement. Be sure to reflect your relationship as it stands right now—not in the distant past!

1. I try to never keep my partner waiting.

2. I make it a point to compliment my partner's appearance.

3. I have a pet name for my partner.

4. My partner and I have a song that is "our song."

5. I like to tell the story of how we met.

6. I handwrite love notes to my partner.

7. I say "I love you" when I leave a phone message.

8. I suggest new activities we can try together.

9. I have cooked my partner a special meal.

10. I go to romantic movies with my partner.

11. I have planned a weekend getaway for the two of us.

12. I share the remote control.

13. I would never agree that my partner should "lose five pounds."

14. I very often say "thank you."

15. I give back rubs.

16. I give foot rubs.

17. I try to look my best when we're out together.

18. I know my partner's favorite flower.

19. I know my partner's favorite sports teams.

20. I refrain from saying, "I told you so."

21. I turn off my cell phone in the bedroom.

22. We often hold hands.

23. I bring my partner little gifts for no particular occasion.

24. We like to snuggle.

25. We like to play footsie under the table.

26. I like to give my partner a wink.

27. I like to give my partner a smile.

28. We have private jokes that only we "get."

29. I've taken my partner on a horse and buggy ride.

30. I do not give household appliances for my partner's birthday.

31. I know my partner's favorite kind of chocolate.

32. I bring home delicacies my partner enjoys.

33. I tell my partner he smells good.

34. I kiss my partner in public.

35. I know my partner's astrological sign.

36. I feel proud to have my partner on my arm.

37. We take walks together.

38. We hug.

39. I make our time together a priority.

40. We love to share a private laugh.

41. I wear clothing I know my partner likes to see me in.

42. We like to sit by a fireside together.

43. We have some meals by candlelight.

44. I look forward to Valentine's Day.

45. I look forward to anniversaries.

46. My partner and I use made-up words or baby talk.

47. I never put my partner on "hold."

48. I enjoy watching my partner sleep (snoring or not).

49. I know my partner's clothing and shoe sizes.

50. I tell my partner how lucky I am to have her in my life—and I believe it.

Scoring and Explanation

Tally your points:

◆ **A score of 40–50** indicates you are very romantic. Your partner is lucky—and so are you, because you have never forgotten the thrill and the fun of falling in love. No matter how hectic life gets, you understand where your priorities are.

◆ **A score of 26–39** indicates you are somewhat romantic. Your relationship is a priority for you, and you enjoy it. No doubt your partner does, too. But hey, if you want to turn up the lovey-dovey factor a little bit, she most likely would be tickled.

◆ **A score of 25 or below** suggests that you could stand to get back in touch with your "inner romantic." It's in there somewhere! If you're interested in adding gusto to your love life, don't be afraid to get a little "schmaltzy." You'll be glad you did, and you won't be the only one celebrating.

19

How Considerate Am I?

Are you a thoughtful sort? Do you make the one you love your number one? Or are you as wrapped up in yourself as a pig in a blanket? Now, now—it's true that might sound harsh. But sometimes after we've been in a relationship for a while, we start taking our mate for granted. When that happens we may fail to be as considerate as we should be.

The reality is that the better we treat our partner, the better he will treat us. So being thoughtful is a win/win. Take this quiz to find out if you're a winner.

Take the Test

Pick the letter that applies to you:

1. When there is one cookie left in the jar, I ...

    A. Leave it for my partner.

    B. Buy or bake more cookies.

    C. Eat it.

2. When the Sunday paper comes, I ...

    A. Share it.

    B. Make sure to give my partner her favorite section first.

    C. Hoard it all until I'm done.

3. When my partner's family comes for dinner, I ...

    A. Keep a stiff upper lip.

    B. Am charming and gracious.

    C. Work late.

4. When a gift-giving occasion comes along, I ...

    A. Ask my partner what she wants.

    B. Have already figured out what my partner would like.

    C. Hope somebody reminds me to get a gift.

5. When my partner is sick, I ...

    A. Ask her what she needs from the drug store.

    B. Make chicken soup, bring her warm blankets, and lay on the TLC.

    C. Avoid her like the plague.

6. If my partner hates to do a particular household chore, I ...

    A. Offer to take turns doing it.

    B. Do it all the time.

    C. Explain how I can't do it or I will throw my back out.

7. I would bring my partner breakfast in bed …

   A. On a special occasion.

   B. Just because.

   C. If she broke both her legs.

8. If my partner went on a weight-loss diet …

   A. I'd eat what he ate whenever we dined together.

   B. I'd help shop for and cook what he was eating.

   C. I'd get to eat all her Valentine's chocolates!

9. When my partner wants to watch a different TV show than I do, I …

   A. Watch what she wants, or negotiate.

   B. Say, "Who needs TV?" and make passionate love to her.

   C. Ask him to watch the small non–HD set in the basement.

10. When my partner wants to eat a new type of cuisine, I …

    A. Give it a try.

    B. Learn how to cook it.

    C. Claim I'm allergic to it.

11. When my partner makes a dumb mistake, I …

    A. Remind her we're all human.

    B. Remind her of all the smart things she's done.

    C. Say, "I told you so."

12. When I am getting romantic with my partner and the phone rings, I …

    A. Let the machine get it.

    B. Wouldn't know because I've turned the ringer off.

    C. Answer it.

13. If I have to cancel dinner plans with my partner, I ...

    A. Send flowers, apologize, and reschedule.

    B. Must have been hit by a truck, because nothing else could keep me away.

    C. Feel hungry and order myself a pizza.

14. When my partner is going to the airport, I ...

    A. Arrange for a car.

    B. Drive her myself.

    C. Remind her to park in the cheap lot.

15. If my partner dropped a contact lens, I'd ...

    A. Crawl around and help him find it.

    B. Help him find it, but reassure him he looks just as cute in glasses.

    C. Say, "Oops, too bad!"

Scoring and Explanation

Tally your total number of "A" responses, "B" responses, and "C" responses:

◆ **A majority of "B" responses** indicates that you are extremely considerate. You put your mate first, and in so doing continually strengthen your bond.

◆ **A majority of "A" responses** indicates that you are a pretty thoughtful mate. You're a good egg and your relationship will most likely never show any cracks.

◆ **A majority of "C" responses** suggests that you are not especially considerate. You may not be completely thoughtless—but most of your thoughts are about yourself. Remember, kindness is a two-way street. You give; you get. Try it sometime.

How Sensual Am I?

Sensuality is exactly what it sounds like. It relates to our five senses: sight, hearing, touch, taste, and smell. Those who are highly sensual relish experiencing sensations. They like to *look*, not merely *see*; they like to *listen*, not merely *hear*; they like to *feel*, not merely *touch*.

Being sensual is not the same as being sexual. However, sensuality is related to our propensity to enjoy the process of sex. Sensual people may have sexual encounters that last longer and that involve more foreplay and afterplay. As a result, they may feel closer to their partners than those who view sex as more of a primal physical release.

Your level of sensuality may also relate to how attractive you are to members of the opposite sex. Sensuality can be a seductive trait, as it tends to signal that someone will be a lover who is interested in pleasing as well as being pleased.

Do you embody and radiate an air of sensuality? You may think so. Take this assessment to learn more.

Take the Test

For each of the following statements, indicate the number of the statement that corresponds to your level of agreement or disagreement:

---

1. Strongly disagree

2. Somewhat disagree

3. Feel neutral or are not sure

4. Somewhat agree

5. Strongly agree

---

1. To me, certain smells bring back distant memories in a flash.

2. The mere thought of a favorite food can make my mouth water.

3. Listening to music can easily affect my mood.

4. I enjoy wearing fabrics that feel soft and smooth against my skin.

5. I love the aroma of good food simmering on the stove.

6. I eat to live rather than live to eat.

7. I can get very drawn in when looking at a work of art.

8. I notice what fabrics and colors other people are wearing.

9. I love the scent of my partner's hair and skin.

10. I like looking through kaleidoscopes.

11. I am a very self-conscious dancer.

12. I enjoy looking at the moon and stars.

13. I like walking barefoot on sand or grass.

14. I like spicy and aromatic foods.

15. I like being massaged.

16. I appreciate the scent of fresh flowers.

17. I don't typically pet animals.

18. I enjoy being nude.

19. I take long baths.

20. I carefully choose the scent of my soap or shower gel.

21. I enjoy the feeling of the breeze in my hair or against my skin.

22. I like bubble baths.

23. I enjoy watching athletes or dancers who move gracefully.

24. I am a very neat eater.

25. I enjoy giving massages.

26. I make appreciative noises when I eat something delectable.

27. I can be very moved by live music.

28. I think all coffees/teas taste pretty much the same.

29. I enjoy taking a dip in a hot tub.

30. I wouldn't enjoy riding in a convertible with the top down.

31. I have a good memory for visual details.

32. I have a hearty laugh.

33. I like hugging and being hugged.

34. I enjoy basking in the sunshine.

35. I am very disciplined about not overindulging in pleasures.

36. I enjoy reading novels or poetry.

37. I love the smell of a new-mown lawn.

38. I enjoy hearing birdsongs.

39. Sad movies never make me cry.

39. I notice the lines and cut of clothing.

40. I think most people need to have more fun.

41. I am very disturbed by unpleasant or annoying noises, e.g., car alarms or dripping faucets.

42. I'd consider skinny-dipping.

43. I like snuggling with my partner.

44. I am very sensate to different kinds of lighting, e.g., fluorescent versus incandescent.

45. I can easily recall some of my all-time favorite meals.

46. I eat very quickly.

47. I enjoy stretching my body.

48. Animals seem to like me.

49. I'd enjoy taking a sauna or steam bath.

50. I try to live in the moment.

Scoring and Explanation

Before tallying your total points, be sure to *reverse the score* (5 = 1, 4 = 2, 3 = 3, 2 = 4, 1 = 5) *for the following items:* 6, 11, 17, 24, 28, 30, 35, 39, 46. Remember, in reversing the score, high numbers are traded for low and vice versa. Unless you reverse the scores for the items listed—and *only* for the items listed—your result will be inaccurate. See the Introduction to this book for a full explanation of reverse scoring.

Tally your points:

◆ **A score of 201–250** indicates that you are highly sensual. You are very "present" in your environment and very attuned to all kinds of sensory input. You also have a strong aesthetic sense. You are probably a lover who takes your time and relishes the act of love-making as much as you relish other bodily delights. If you are on the very high end of the scale (above 225), you might be someone who needs to rein in your lust for pleasure some of the time, lest you fall prey to overindulgent hedonism.

◆ **A score of 165–200** indicates that you have a moderate degree of sensuality. You might be more selectively sensual than someone who scores higher. For example, you might be highly attuned to tactile or visual stimulation, but not have an acute sense of smell.

To up your pleasure quotient in life and in love, notice the areas where you are sensual, and allow yourself to experience pleasures related to them.

◆ **A score of 164 or below** suggests that you are not very sensual. Or perhaps you are simply resistant to giving in to your sensual impulses because they make you feel guilty or uncomfortably exposed. If your pragmatic approach to life is a sore spot between you and your partner, see if you are willing to explore a few indulgences within the context of a safe, loving relationship. Maybe you've never tried a massage or lit a scented candle. You'll never know your reaction until you *do* try.

Note: In general, women should expect to score higher on this assessment than men—though there are, of course, exceptions. Whether women are "wired" to be more appreciative of sensation than men or whether they are simply given more social reinforcement in this area than men is up for debate—as are just about all matters of gender difference.

Am I Sex Savvy?

Sex is a natural part of life. We wouldn't be here without it. Yet many of us know less about sex and matters related to sexuality than we do about other natural parts of life—say, food. That's unfortunate, because human sexuality is an endlessly fascinating topic.

The following test is not a determinant of whether or not you're a good lover, but rather of how much you have indulged your curiosity about sex. It is designed for entertainment and for learning purposes. So, don't be embarrassed or shy. Go for it! And, to add some extra excitement, try taking the test with your partner.

Take the Test

Indicate the letter of the response you believe is correct:

1. According to the 2007 Durex Sexual Well-Being Global Survey, how many times a year does the average American have sex?

    A. 85

    B. 52

    C. 156

2. What is the Kama Sutra?

    A. A currylike spice reputed to be an aphrodisiac.

    B. An ancient Sanskrit guide to love and sexual pleasures.

    C. A vibrator featured on *Sex and the City*.

3. According to Dr. Mehmet Oz, what is the percentage of women who routinely experience multiple orgasms?

    A. 50 percent

    B. 90 percent

    C. 15 percent

4. Why are women's bodies better equipped for multiple orgasms than are men's bodies?

    A. Men's heart rates need more time to stabilize after one orgasm.

    B. Women's brains release more endorphins during sex.

    C. Blood engorges a casing around the male organ that can't refill for a while.

5. The period of time it takes a male to be able to climax again after one orgasm is called …

    A. The recovery period.

    B. The refractory period.

    C. The "Hey, what's on TV?" period.

6. What is the length of the average erect male penis?

    A. 3–4 inches

    B. 5–7 inches

    C. 9–10 inches

7. Males with largish nonerect penises achieve a 75 percent increase in size during erection. What percentage of increase do men with smaller nonerect penises achieve?

    A. 75 percent

    B. 50 percent

    C. 100 percent

8. What is the G-spot?

    A. The tip of the clitoris

    B. An erogenous zone on the inner upper wall of the vagina

    C. A wife-swapping club

9. Massage of the male prostate gland is said to produce intense orgasms. Where is the gland?

    A. At the base of the penis

    B. Adjacent to the rectum

    C. In the testes

10. How many calories does a teaspoon of male ejaculate contain?

    A. 5–7

    B. 50–60

    C. 200–225

11. Signs that a woman is experiencing a climax include all of the following *except* ...

    A. Flushed face and ears.

    B. Erect nipples.

    C. Rapid breathing.

    D. Reduced body temperature.

    E. A stiffening body.

12. Techniques of Tantric sex, which is rooted in Eastern spiritual philosophy, include all of the following *except* ...

    A. Breath control.

    B. Eye contact.

    C. Accelerated foreplay.

    D. Start and stop techniques.

    E. A variety of positions.

13. Which scent has research shown is a sexual turn on for American men?

    A. Buttered popcorn

    B. Hot dogs

    C. Pumpkin pie

14. Whose 1948 book on sex research prompted *Time* magazine to declare, "Not since *Gone With the Wind* had booksellers seen anything like it"?

    A. Masters and Johnson

    B. Alfred Kinsey

    C. Dr. Ruth

15. A popular ad campaign was based on the widespread rumor contending that which of the following substances had widespread aphrodisiac effects?

    A. Dove soap

    B. Hershey's kisses

    C. Green M&Ms

16. The fact that bananas, cucumbers, and asparagus all have an aphrodisiac reputation in folklore is due to ...

    A. Their pungent aromas.

    B. Their phallic shapes.

    C. Their high potassium content.

17. At what age are women supposed to reach their sexual peak?

    A. Late thirties

    B. Late teens

    C. Mid fifties

18. According to the 2007 Durex Sexual Well-Being Global Survey, which group has sex most frequently?

    A. Brazilians

    B. Greeks

    C. The British

19. According to Sari Locker, author of *The Complete Idiot's Guide to Amazing Sex, Third Edition* (Alpha Books, 2005), what is the main problem that is probably behind many of the problems in American's sex life?

    A. Fatigue

    B. Strained relationships

    C. Lack of time

20. According to an *Esquire* magazine survey, 61 percent of which gender say they would rather give up sex than lose sleep?

    A. Women

    B. Men

    C. Both women and men

Scoring and Explanation

Assign yourself one point for each of your answers that match the following answer key:

1. A	6. B	11. D	16. B
2. B	7. C	12. C	17. A
3. C	8. B	13. C	18. B
4. C	9. B	14. B	19. C
5. B	10. A	15. C	20. A

◆ **A score of 17–20** indicates you know a lot about sexuality. You are probably comfortable with your sexuality and curious about human sexuality in a healthy way.

◆ **A score of 13–16** indicates a moderate degree of knowledge. Just the fact that you took this quiz means you are open to knowing more on the subject. I hope you picked up some interesting tidbits.

◆ **A score of 12 or below** suggests you should not choose the "Sexuality" category on *Jeopardy*. But take heart. There are many good books available on sexuality. It's never too late to read them and then take a "practical exam."

Quiz **22**

How Dependent Am I?

All romantic partnerships—indeed all close relationships—presume a certain level of *interdependence*. Both parties rely mutually upon one another for various kinds of support, be it emotional, social, or financial. And both parties benefit from this arrangement.

Interdependence is a healthy relationship dynamic. Indeed, without it, there's not much of a relationship at all. But sometimes dependence can become lopsided. If one individual is too dependent on another, both parties may come to resent the arrangement. The partner who is overly depended upon may feel burdened. But, just as significantly, the one who depends too much on the other may feel diminished.

How dependent are you on your partner? Take the test and find out.

Take the Test

For each of the following statements, indicate the number of the statement that corresponds to your level of agreement or disagreement:

1. Strongly disagree

2. Somewhat disagree

3. Feel neutral or are not sure

4. Somewhat agree

5. Strongly agree

1. I rarely make any social plans without consulting my partner.

2. I rarely make any social plans that do not include my partner.

3. I prefer that my partner handle all major financial decisions.

4. I tend to blame my partner whenever things go wrong.

5. I won't wear any outfit my partner dislikes.

6. I enjoy doing some things on my own.

7. I enjoy participating in some activities with friends—without my partner being present.

8. I would never dream of voting for a candidate my partner did not support.

9. I feel insecure when my partner spends time with friends and does not include me.

10. I like to know where my partner is at all times.

11. I make sure my partner is always aware of my whereabouts.

12. I feel uncomfortable if my partner travels without me for business.

13. I have taken or would consider taking a vacation without my partner.

14. I rely on my partner to keep tabs on my diet or other health matters.

15. My partner makes my doctor's appointments for me.

16. I have trouble sleeping if my partner is not beside me.

17. I count on my partner to fix things around the house.

18. I count on my partner to do the bulk of the housecleaning.

19. I would never shop for or cook food my partner dislikes—even if I really like it.

20. I feel nervous or shy at social events without my partner at my side.

21. I won't buy a style of clothing my partner does not like.

22. I am more of a leader than a follower.

23. I believe my partner is the only person who could possibly ever understand the "real" me.

24. I frequently think about how lost I would be without my partner.

25. I fear displeasing my partner in any way.

26. I fear my partner abandoning me.

27. I believe my partner is much better off with me than without me.

28. I am generally a people pleaser.

29. I would never contradict my partner in public.

30. I give in easily in arguments with my partner.

31. I believe people form judgments of me based on what they think of my partner.

32. I say "we" far more often than I say "I."

33. I monitor my partner's health extremely closely.

34. I often fear what would happen if my partner became ill.

35. I believe I could never survive financially without my partner.

36. I have some friends my partner is not crazy about.

37. I avoid members of my own family if my partner does not care for them.

38. My partner is the parent who always disciplines our kids.

39. I will try something new even if my partner is not interested.

40. I would rather be alone with my partner than socialize with other couples.

Scoring and Explanation

Before tallying your total points, be sure to *reverse the score* (5 = 1, 4 = 2, 3 = 3, 2 = 4, 1 = 5) *for the following items*: 6, 7, 13, 22, 27, 36, 39. Remember, in reversing the score, high numbers are traded for low and vice versa. Unless you reverse the scores for the items listed—and *only* for the items listed—your result will be inaccurate. See the Introduction to this book for a full explanation of reverse scoring.

Tally your points:

◆ **A score of 151–200** indicates that you are highly dependent on your partner. While interdependence is a sure sign of a strong bond, you could actually be weakening your bond by being overly reliant. Relationships actually thrive when both parties share responsibility. What's more, there is something to be said for piquing your partner's interest in you by doing more things on your own. When he asks, "What did you do today?" let him be surprised with your answer once in a while. Pursuing some things independently makes you more interesting and enables you to contribute more to your life as a couple.

◆ **A score of 101–150** indicates that you are optimally interdependent with your partner. Yours appears to be a relationship of give and take. You rely on your partner, and you take her needs into account; however, you do not apportion undue power to her. You are capable of making decisions, and you trust yourself to do so. You know you could survive on your own—even though you'd rather not! You probably have a healthy level of self-regard, and this is an attractive quality that will keep your partner intrigued with you.

◆ **A score of 100 or below** suggests that you are highly independent with your partner. While self-reliance is good up to a point, consider whether you might be sending your partner the message that you do not need her—and perhaps do not care about her well-being as much as she would like. You probably do not mean to do this, but be aware that this is a potential pitfall of your extreme self-sufficiency. There is no need to be joined at the hip, but it wouldn't hurt to let her know that you genuinely value her input and, of course, her company.

23

Do I Fight Fair?

All couples disagree now and then. You and your partner might have some differing goals or differing ideas about how to reach those goals. Or you might have legitimate gripes abut how you're being treated. Or you might just be in a cranky mood. None of these are reason to throw in the towel. There is no such thing as a conflict-free relationship—at least, not if it is a close and genuine relationship.

It's not a question of "if" but rather of "how" you fight that determines whether or not your relationship can withstand the occasional argument. The following quiz will help you assess whether or not you fight fair, or hit below the proverbial belt.

Take the Test

Circle all of those that apply to you:

When I argue with my partner, I am likely to …

1. Reply to an accusation with a counteraccusation.

2. Bring up past problems and conflicts.

3. Shout.

4. Call him names.

5. Swear.

6. Cry.

7. Storm out in the middle of a quarrel.

8. Threaten to leave the relationship.

9. Criticize her parents, siblings, or friends when the argument is not primarily about her.

10. Begin sentences with "you."

11. Clam up in midargument and refuse to say more.

12. Fight in public.

13. Argue in front of the kids.

14. Fight about the same things over and over.

15. Give him the silent treatment afterward.

Scoring and Explanation

Simply count the number of items you circled:

◆ **If you circled none of the above**—and you're being scrupulously honest—then you are a paragon, a virtual Mohandas Gandhi of relationship-fighting. You either instinctively understand, or have learned over time, that voicing a difference of opinion does not require being provocative, disrespectful, or histrionic. Assuming you are expressing your needs appropriately—as opposed to stifling any discontent you feel—your relationship will benefit from your ability to keep a cool head.

◆ **If you circled one or two items**, you're a pretty fair fighter overall. Look at the one or two items you circled and see if you can moderate your behavior in these areas. If you are able to accomplish this, your partner will *hear* your point of view even more clearly, because she will not have to be in the defensive.

◆ **If you circled between three and five items**, you need to work on your temper and your impulsivity during arguments. No fair saying that your partner "stirs you up." You have to take responsibility for your own tactics. Only by changing the way you respond within the context of a relationship can you change the dynamics of that relationship.

◆ **If you circled more than five items**, hold on to your seat belt—it's going to be a bumpy relationship (and very possibly a disintegrating one) until and unless you get a handle on how you react during conflict.

Quiz 24

Is My Fate with My Mate?

Does your relationship seem suited for the long haul? Are you likely to be in it for better, worse, richer, poorer ... you know, the whole 18 holes? If so, you'll need more than passion and sexual attraction. Commitment and emotional intimacy are required as well.

Long-term relationships mandate a healthy dose of respect, patience, and affection. Not to mention a good sense of humor. Take the following quiz to see if your relationship has what it takes to sustain itself through life's ups, downs, and in-betweens.

Take the Test

For each of the following statements, indicate the number of the statement that corresponds to your level of agreement or disagreement:

1. Strongly disagree

2. Somewhat disagree

3. Feel neutral or are not sure (or is inapplicable)

4. Somewhat agree

5. Strongly agree

1. My partner is my friend as well as my lover.

2. We have a lot of physical chemistry between us.

3. We share similar long-term goals.

4. I would gladly make sacrifices for my partner.

5. My partner and I enjoy traveling together.

6. My partner really understands me.

7. Our kids take priority over our relationship.

8. I find my partner beautiful/handsome.

9. I am capable of putting my partner's happiness before my own.

10. My partner accepts my shortcomings without judgment.

11. I like my partner's friends.

12. My partner says "yes" when he means "no."

13. We share a similar sense of humor.

14. I feel like I do more to maintain the relationship than my partner does.

15. My partner and I are tolerant of one another's parents, brothers, and sisters.

16. My partner is capable of putting me first.

17. We enjoy trying new things together.

18. One of us is a workaholic (or both of us are workaholics).

19. I consider my partner my soulmate.

20. We make sure we have quality time to spend together.

21. My partner's positive attributes far outweigh her flaws.

22. I sometimes suspect my partner is hiding something important.

23. My partner is a good parent (or I believe he will be a good parent).

24. I keep many secrets from my partner.

25. If we argue, we make up quickly.

Scoring and Explanation

Before tallying your total points, be sure to *reverse the score* (5 = 1, 4 = 2, 3 = 3, 2 = 4, 1 = 5) *for the following items:* 7, 12, 14, 18, 22, 24. Remember, in reversing the score, high numbers are traded for low and vice versa. Unless you reverse the scores for the items listed—and *only* for the items listed—your result will be inaccurate. See the Introduction to this book for a full explanation of reverse scoring.

Tally your points:

◆ **A score of 98–125** indicates that your relationship has definite staying power. You have a respectful, loving attitude toward your partner, and you should have many years of contentment ahead.

◆ **A score of 85–97** means that you have a serious shot at relationship longevity, although you might have a few bumps in the road. Look at any items on which you scored 1 or 2, and resolve to explore the issues they suggest. This preventive strategy should help you to seal your fate with your mate.

◆ **A score below 85** suggests that your relationship needs some tender loving care if it is to withstand the test of time. If you are nursing grudges or holding on to doubts, you will have to face up to what may be unspoken. But don't panic, or "throw the baby out with the bathwater." Reflect on what you consider are the problems in the relationship and perhaps even consider enlisting professional assistance.

Note: This quiz included two items related to parenthood. If you and your partner have children, it bodes well for the relationship if you respect one another's parenting skills. On the other hand, it does not bode well if you both consistently ignore one another's needs in order to put the children's needs first. Marriage typically follows a *U-shaped curve of marital happiness:* newlywed contentment ebbs with the arrival of children, and then hits a nadir when a couple has adolescent children at home. But once the children leave the nest, a couple's level of satisfaction typically rises again. Raising capable and well-adjusted children is a laudable joint endeavor, but don't put all your eggs in the parenting basket. Once they're launched, you and your partner still have many years of couplehood ahead.

4

My Personality with Friends, Neighbors, and Others

In this part of the book, you evaluate some traits that are apt to impact your social life. Do you project an aura of friendliness, or give off a "keep away" vibe? Are you skilled at understanding other people's points of view—or would you rather just control them? Are you a do-gooder? A loner? A laugh riot? And, finally, are you an ideal friend of felines or a compassionate canine companion?

25

Am I Approachable?

Some folks are "people people." They're genuinely curious about others and willing to give strangers the benefit of the doubt. They like everyone—at least until someone proves himself to be unlikable. Their friendly, open attitude is communicated in various ways to people all around them. Consequently they become virtual people magnets.

Other people might as well be walking around with "Do not disturb" signs hung around their necks. They seem to give off an aura that says, "Don't come hither." Their manner inspires others to give them a wide berth.

Which type are you? Take the quiz and see.

Take the Test

For each of the following statements, indicate the number that corresponds to the level of frequency with which you behave as the statement describes:

1. Never

2. Rarely

3. Sometimes

4. Often

1. I have a ready smile.

2. I make eye contact with people.

3. I've been known to eavesdrop on conversations of people around me.

4. In spare moments, I have my nose in a book, newspaper, or magazine.

5. I've stopped on the street to sign a petition or to give money.

6. I am pleased with my physical appearance.

7. I walk around wearing headphones.

8. I am a people watcher.

9. I have helped a stranger in need.

10. I engage in small talk.

11. I give compliments.

12. I expose myself to different points of view.

13. I am not interested in other people's problems.

14. I find myself at a loss for words.

15. I am self-conscious.

16. I have been complimented on my sense of humor.

17. I feel pressed for time.

18. People come to me for advice.

19. I am good at making people feel at ease.

20. I find it hard to relax.

Scoring and Explanation

Before tallying your total points, be sure to *reverse the score* (4 = 1, 3 = 2, 2 = 3, 1 = 4) *for the following items:* 4, 7, 13, 14, 15, 17, 20. Remember, in reversing the score, high numbers are traded for low and vice versa. Unless you reverse the scores for the items listed—and *only* for the items listed—your result will be inaccurate. See the Introduction to this book for a full explanation of reverse scoring.

Tally your points:

◆ **A score of 66–80** indicates that you are approachable. You appear to be open and agreeable: a "people person." These characteristics make people feel it is safe to interact with you—whether it's to ask for directions or to begin—at least potentially—a deeper relationship. Odds are you have many friends and affable relationships with everyone from co-workers and neighbors to the cashiers at your local supermarket and the tellers at your bank.

◆ **A score of 55–65** indicates that you are somewhat approachable. Your level of openness and agreeableness is probably contingent on the specific situation you are in, as well as the mood you are in. There are times when you give "Come hither" signals, and other times when your manner says "Keep away." There's nothing wrong with that, but it's always a good idea to be sure you are aware of what signals you're giving off when. If you want to be approached, make a conscious effort to emerge from your "own little world."

◆ **A score of 54 or below** suggests you are not very approachable. And maybe that's just the way you like it! You tend to be suspicious of strangers, and impatient with people in general. On the bright side, you'll rarely get a cold because few people can get close enough to you to spread their germs.

But seriously, if you'd like to be more approachable, notice the cues you are giving off that are working against you. Are you walking around with a grimace on your face? Are you cocooning in public—all wrapped in your iPod and your daily paper? Don't expect to break out of your cocoon and become a butterfly overnight, but try flashing a smile once in a while. You might meet someone who changes your less-than-sterling opinion of your fellow humans.

26

What's My Humor Aptitude?

The ability to appreciate and to share humor is a trait that creates many beneficial effects. A hearty laugh brings an immediate physical release of tension. Laughter is a form of *eustress*—positive stress (that's "eu" as in euphoria). Unlike *dis*tress or negative stress, it makes us feel vibrant and "up." As it bubbles up, laughter stimulates the brain, the nervous system, the respiratory system, the hormonal system, and the muscular system. It releases feel-good *endorphins* in the brain. And it's a pretty good aerobic workout to boot.

But that's not all. Humor offers us a way to create rapport, bond emotionally with others, and strengthen our social connections. Perhaps most significantly, humor can help us rise above our worries and frustrations. It helps us maintain perspective and re-evaluate negative circumstances in a more positive light. Humor can help create optimism, and it can help us rebound from crises more quickly than we otherwise might have.

So how's your sense of humor? Are you often in a frame of mind to give laughter a chance to work its magic? The following assessment will help you find out.

Take the Test

For each of the following statements, indicate the number that corresponds to the level of frequency with which you behave as the statement describes:

1. Never

2. Rarely

3. Sometimes

4. Often

1. When something strikes me as funny, I laugh out loud.

2. There are certain movies or TV shows I can always count on to make me laugh.

3. I can find a humorous aspect to a frustrating situation.

4. I enjoy the company of witty people.

5. I feel self-conscious when I am laughing.

6. I have been told I have a good sense of humor.

7. I feel warm toward people with whom I share laughter.

8. I have favorite comedians who can always make me laugh.

9. I enjoy many kinds of humor, from slapstick to satire.

10. I laugh out loud several times during the course of the day.

11. My friends and I share a similar sense of humor.

12. I have laughed so hard it's brought tears to my eyes.

13. In a stressful situation, I think about what a juicy anecdote I'll have to tell later.

14. I enjoy looking at political cartoons.

15. I am wary of people who seem to have no sense of humor.

16. I think it's always wrong to poke fun at serious subjects.

17. When others are laughing, I often don't "get" what's so funny.

18. I enjoy reading the work of humorous writers.

19. I enjoy hearing the sound of laughter.

20. I tend to socialize in groups.

21. Some of my best friends are genuinely funny.

22. My pets make me laugh.

23. My kids make me laugh.

24. I have had to suppress a giggle fit in a public situation.

25. I did best in classes when the teachers had a sense of humor.

26. I am capable of laughing at myself.

27. I enjoy making a crowd of people laugh.

28. I think people look attractive when they are laughing.

29. People tell me I should "lighten up."

30. I am attracted to members of the opposite sex who are witty.

31. Exposure to something funny puts me in a better mood.

32. I'm a funny storyteller.

33. I've been in situations where laughter seemed contagious.

34. I carefully memorize jokes, but find it hard to be spontaneously funny.

35. I come up with funny comments "off the top of my head."

Scoring and Explanation

Before tallying your total points, be sure to *reverse the score* (4 = 1, 3 = 2, 2 = 3, 1 = 4) *for the following items:* 5, 16, 17, 29, 34. Remember, in reversing the score, high numbers are traded for low and vice versa. Unless you reverse the scores for the items listed—and *only* for the items listed—your result will be inaccurate. See the Introduction to this book for a full explanation of reverse scoring.

Tally your points:

◆ **A score of 125–140** indicates that you have a high humor aptitude. You like to laugh and you often create opportunities to do
so. You surround yourself with witty people and put yourself in
circumstances where humor can work its therapeutic magic. Hold
on to your sense of humor. It is a precious resource.

◆ **A score of 105–124** indicates that you have a moderate humor
aptitude. You like to laugh and appreciate wit, but perhaps you
are too preoccupied to look on the lighter side as much as you
could. To up your eustress through humor, try putting together
a "humor library" that you can turn to in times when you need
a lift. Collect your favorite funny DVDs, CDs, and books. Put
them in a central location—perhaps bedside—where you can
easily access them when you could use a change of perspective,
not to mention an endorphin boost.

◆ **A score of 104 or below** suggests you could stand to lighten up.
(I'm guessing this is not the first time you've heard this!) There is
certainly a time to be serious, but your serious side could be veer-
ing toward somber. No one expects you to morph into a stand-up
comedian, but do look for opportunities where you can be, if not
the life of the party, then at least a party guest. Take this advice
literally. Your problem *could* be that you are not spending enough
time in the company of others. Simply socializing in large groups
on a more regular basis can get your laugh quotient way up.

Note: Experts say the average American adult laughs 15 times a day.
However, some stress researchers suggest we need at least 20 daily
laughs to alleviate our angst. If you suspect you are laugh-deprived, at
least in the statistical sense, try keeping a Laughter Log for a week. Put
a check mark in your day planner every time you giggle or guffaw; then
tally them up, and see where you stand.

27

How Altruistic Am I?

Altruism has long been defined as the inclination to perform unselfish actions that benefit others. But as essayist, philosopher, and poet Ralph Waldo Emerson wrote, "It is one of the most beautiful compensations of this life that no man can sincerely try to help another without helping himself ...." Contemporary research proves Emerson correct. Helping others does indeed benefit the giver as well as the recipient.

An overwhelming convergence of social science research supports the hypothesis that benevolent attitudes and actions focused on the good of others contribute to the happiness, health, and even longevity of the *giver* (while in no way diminishing benefits to the recipient).

According to Dr. Stephen G. Post, Ph.D., a preeminent Case Western University researcher in this field and author of the book *Why Good Things Happen to Good People* (see the Appendix), "Everyday kindness and good deeds ... bestow upon the giver a feeling of meaning, buoyancy, and warmth." Moreover, focusing positive attention on others appears to contribute to emotional and physical well-being that can add years to one's life. This is, at least in part, because the feelings of accomplishment and security that one obtains from doing unto others are significant counterpoints to frustration and stress.

Are you likely to receive the benefits of giving? That depends on how altruistic you are. Take the quiz and find out.

Take the Test

This test has two sections to it. First, for each of the following 20 statements, indicate the number of the statement that corresponds to your level of agreement or disagreement:

1. Strongly disagree

2. Somewhat disagree

3. Feel neutral or are not sure

4. Somewhat agree

5. Strongly agree

When you complete this part, follow the directions for the next section, which will involve responding to some hypothetical scenarios:

1. I do favors for others without being asked.

2. Helping others is a good use of my time.

3. I am likely to help a complete stranger I'll never see again.

4. I am most likely to help in a situation where I know I am being watched by others.

5. I am thought of as someone people can turn to when they need help.

6. I am very innovative when it comes to figuring out ways to be helpful.

7. I don't need people to make a big deal out of the help I give them.

8. If someone else is around when help is needed, I leave it to her to provide assistance.

9. I have mentored a younger person.

10. I will only help someone who can potentially do something for me.

11. If no one else is helping, why should I?

12. I live by the Golden Rule: "Do unto others as you would have others do unto you."

13. I would inconvenience myself to help a friend.

14. Donating to charity is a priority for me.

15. I do not like the feeling of owing someone a favor.

16. I donate blood on a regular basis.

17. Helping others makes me feel good about myself.

18. The more I get, the more I give.

19. I engage in activities that help my community.

20. I engage in activities that I believe help humanity in general.

Now, for the following four scenarios, indicate whether you would or would not perform the action in question. Simply note "yes" or "no." If you are not sure, that counts as a "no."

1. You come into a significant unexpected sum of money, and are asked to immediately donate 25 percent of it to a worthy cause. The money you donate would appreciably benefit your community in an important way. The only catch is, you would have to donate the money anonymously. Would you do it?

2. You are walking along a beautiful and apparently unspoiled beach when you come across a pile of trash. The trash is about 100 yards from a trash receptacle. No one else is around. Would you carry the trash to the receptacle?

3. You notice that a co-worker has made a mistake in some calculation that, if uncaught at this stage, will ultimately lead him to make an embarrassing public blunder. You can correct his mistake, but if you do, you will get no credit for it. Will you?

4. You are driving to an important meeting when you come across a stranded vehicle on an otherwise deserted road. The driver of the vehicle is alone and has fashioned a sign that says: "Help. No cell phone." Do you stop to assist even if being late could jeopardize the success of your meeting?

Scoring and Explanation

To obtain the first part of your score, tally your points. But before doing so, be sure to *reverse the score* (5 = 1, 4 = 2, 3 = 3, 2 = 4, 1 = 5) *for the following items:* 4, 8, 10, 11, 15. Remember, in reversing the score, high numbers are traded for low and vice versa. Unless you reverse the scores for the items listed—and *only* for the items listed—your result will be inaccurate. See the Introduction to this book for a full explanation of reverse scoring.

To obtain the second part of your score, give yourself 5 points for each scenario to which you responded "yes."

Add the two parts of your score together to get your final result:

◆ **A score of 85–100** indicates that you are highly altruistic. You embody an attitude of kindness and are disposed to put that attitude into action. Helping others is a priority for you, and you seem to instinctively understand that putting others first, at least some of the time, is also a way of nurturing yourself. Chances are you consider yourself a happy person, for, as Dr. Albert Schweitzer once remarked, "The only ones among you who will be really happy are those who have sought and found how to serve."

Note: If you have scored at the very high end of this range, it is important that you keep a caveat in mind. Doing unto others to an overwhelming extent, especially if coupled with self-neglect and martyrdom, can lead to burnout; it can create rather than counter stress, and can have negative health effects. Your altruism is admirable and a potential source of joy for you. But you won't be of use to anyone if you are running on empty, so take care to ensure that your own needs are being met along with the needs of others. A lack of self-care reflects a lack of self-acceptance. It could be an indication that your altruism is actually a "cover" for a lack of self-regard. Loving yourself and loving others should go hand in hand.

◆ **A score of 70–84** indicates that you have some altruistic tendencies. You probably notice that you do feel much more satisfied in your life when you are having a positive impact on others, but perhaps you find yourself too preoccupied to be of as much help as you would like. You might consider actively creating more opportunities to serve others. A bit of research in your own community or on the Internet will yield a wealth of ideas about how you can formally volunteer in a way that suits your abilities, interests, and schedule. Beyond that, make it a practice to keep your eyes open for opportunities to assist those in your immediate circle in simple ways. Do a good deed daily and see how it lightens your life.

◆ **A score of 69 or below** suggests that you could use an altruism boost. Remember, helping others is self-help, whereas an attitude of obliviousness toward others' needs actually translates into self-harm. Just ask Ebenezer Scrooge.

Even if you are skeptical about increasing your long-term levels of emotional satisfaction and physical well-being through helping others, try experimenting with altruism on a basic physiological level. Do something for someone and notice the instant warm glow that results. Performing an act of kindness is likely to give your brain a boost of a feel-good chemical called *dopamine*. To do good is—literally—to feel good. Now watch out: this could become habit forming! And while research shows that lifelong benefits accrue to those who began altruistic habits at a young age, it is never too late to get started and to benefit as a result.

28

Am I Alone Too Much?

Perhaps you enjoy spending some quality time with one of your favorite people: you! There is nothing wrong with that. A certain amount of alone time is necessary for restorative purposes. We all need time to relax and regroup. Many creative types also find they need self-enforced solitude when they are writing, painting, composing, or simply allowing their minds to roam freely and remain open to inspiration.

That said, spending too much time by ourselves could deprive us of social support. Social support is a factor proven to decrease harmful stress. (When we respond to others with what psychologists call a *tend and befriend* response, we actually release feel-good hormones into our systems.) Social support also increases emotional and physical well-being, and facilitates happiness and life satisfaction.

No person is an island. We are all interdependent. Are you reaping the benefits of connection, or are you spending too much time keeping your own company?

Take the Test

For each of the following statements, indicate the number that corresponds to how frequently you behave as the statement describes:

1. Never

2. Rarely

3. Sometimes

4. Often

1. I spend time with at least one person who knows the "real" me.

2. I interact with others in a volunteer setting.

3. I make excuses to avoid social events.

4. I belong to a professional group and attend its meetings.

5. I avoid meeting new people.

6. I have called on a friend, family member, or neighbor for help in an emergency.

7. I have called a friend, family member, or neighbor when I needed cheering up.

8. I feel isolated.

9. I go a whole day without speaking to anyone.

10. People find me interesting.

11. My social contacts are superficial.

12. I keep my opinions to myself.

13. I am bored.

14. I play an organized sport.

15. I attend religious services.

16. I enjoy making people laugh.

17. I have trouble figuring out what is expected of me in social situations.

18. I spend holidays or birthdays by myself.

19. When I'm alone, I don't know what to do with myself.

20. I belong to a book club, garden club, or other hobby-related club.

21. I feel sad that people neglect me.

22. I live with one or more pets.

23. I can always find someone to pal around with.

24. I belong to a social-action or fundraising group.

25. I wonder what happened to people I was once close to.

Scoring and Explanation

Before tallying your total points, be sure to *reverse the score* (4 = 1, 3 = 2, 2 = 3, 1 = 4) *for the following items:* 3, 5, 8, 9, 11, 12, 13, 17, 18, 19, 21, 25. Remember, in reversing the score, high numbers are traded for low and vice versa. Unless you reverse the scores for the items listed—and *only* for the items listed—your result will be inaccurate. See the Introduction to this book for a full explanation of reverse scoring.

Tally your points:

◆ **A score of 50 or below** suggests that you may well be spending too much time alone. Time alone, per se, is not a negative thing. Everyone requires downtime, and some people deliberately choose more solitude than others, especially if they like to pursue creative endeavors, reading, meditation, and the like. However, your score indicates that you might be spending more time alone than you wish to and than is beneficial for you.

Perhaps you are not sure what to do about your situation. If you want to break out of what may have become habitual lonely routines, think in terms of expanding your network. Put another way, think in terms of increasing your *social capital*. Social capital is measured by our involvement in groups, organizations, and communities that provide us with opportunities to feel a part of something greater than ourselves. Think about what interests you—from books to bowling, from plants to politics—and look for an organization that focuses on that activity. Think about how you can be useful in your community, and look for a volunteer organization that could put your skills and talents to use. Start slowly, and dip your toe back into the world of social interaction. Notice if your feelings about yourself and your life are enhanced by your new connection. If they are, you are off to a strong start you can build upon.

29

Am I Controlling?

Do you want people to do it your way? Do you think you know best—or at least better than anyone else around you? Most of us want others to do our bidding some of the time, and most of us attempt to control our environment and even to influence the fates to some degree.

But as with most things, controlling behavior can create problems—both interpersonal and intrapersonal—if it goes too far. Take the following assessment to find out just how controlling you tend to be.

Take the Test

For each of the following statements, indicate the number of the statement that corresponds to your level of agreement or disagreement:

1. Strongly disagree

2. Somewhat disagree

3. Feel neutral or are not sure

4. Somewhat agree

5. Strongly agree

1. I insist on taking care of family finances.

2. I have strong opinions.

3. I take the lead in important family decisions.

4. I am punctual.

5. I like neatness and order.

6. I have been described as easygoing.

7. I try to keep a lid on my temper.

8. I am a light sleeper.

9. I am honest at all costs.

10. I have withheld information to get the results I want.

11. People who know me are wary of contradicting me.

12. When shopping, I know what most items should cost.

13. In arguments, I get the last word.

14. I often know what time it is without looking at the clock.

15. I know the calorie or carbohydrate counts of most foods.

16. I've been described as bossy.

17. I never wake up before my alarm clock rings.

18. I am a bargain hunter.

19. I make promises to get people to do what I want.

20. I am nonjudgmental.

21. There are certain foods I won't allow in the house.

22. I know what people around me desire most.

23. I know what people around me fear most.

24. I am persistent when it comes to achieving goals.

25. If I'm too hot or cold, I'll adjust the thermostat rather than change my clothes.

26. I am a natural leader.

27. I am good at assigning tasks.

28. I value clear rules and structure.

29. I hate inefficiency.

30. I hate committees.

31. When I'm on vacation, I relax easily.

32. I am a news junkie.

33. I am a careful proofreader.

34. In my household, I am the one holding the TV's remote control.

35. In my extended family, I am the one my relatives look to to make decisions.

36. I could tell most people how to improve their lives.

37. I dislike taking direction from others.

38. I am never reluctant to admit when I am wrong.

39. I tend to fill my free time with planned activities.

40. You wouldn't want to be someone who stands in my way.

Scoring and Explanation

To obtain the first part of your score, tally your points. But before doing so, be sure to *reverse the score (5 = 1, 4 = 2, 3 = 3, 2 = 4, 1 = 5) for the following items:* 6, 9, 17, 20, 31, 38. Remember, in reversing the score, high numbers are traded for low and vice versa. Unless you reverse the scores for the items listed—and *only* for the items listed—your result will be inaccurate. See the Introduction to this book for a full explanation of reverse scoring.

◆ **A score of 161–200** indicates that you are highly controlling. You believe you know best in nearly all situations, and you find it hard to loosen your grip. You may, in fact, be extremely smart and capable, and very competent when it comes to making decisions. *However*, you might also be alienating those around you. Being controlling can be very damaging to your most valued relationships. Everyone—*not just you*—wants to feel that his or her input is valued. When people feel unappreciated, they start to disengage from you—and sometimes even start to hide things from you.

It's not easy for controllers to change. And the higher your score, the harder change will be. Start small. You'll benefit from relaxing your grip on some little things. Let someone else choose the evening's TV fare or let him select the menu for dinner. You might be surprised at the sense of freedom and discovery that comes from empowering others to let new things into your life. In the end, you really can't control everything—or even most things. Getting used to being more open and spontaneous will make you more resilient and increasingly calm.

◆ **A score of 126–160** indicates that you are somewhat controlling. Most test-takers will probably fall somewhere in this range. Most of us want to exert some leverage over others and to manipulate the outcomes of some situations. There's nothing fundamentally wrong with this impulse. But it is helpful to keep in mind what has come to be known as the *serenity prayer:* "Give me the grace to accept with serenity the things that cannot be changed, courage to change the things that should be changed, and the wisdom to know the difference."

◆ **A score of 125 or below** suggests you are not a controlling type.
This could be because you are a relaxed and easygoing sort, *or*
it could be because you are afraid of confrontation. Think about
what feelings come up for you when you are faced with making a
decision that impacts other people. Are you deferring because you
would genuinely be satisfied with most outcomes? If so, you're just
a happy-go-lucky sort—and you'll probably live a long, healthy life
of contentment. But if you are deferring because you lack confidence and are scared of others' potential disapproval, consider that
you might want to be a bit more assertive.

Quiz 30

Do I Express Enough Gratitude?

A growing body of research shows that people who make a habit of expressing gratitude report feeling increased happiness, energy, and optimism. A 1998 Gallup survey of American adults and teenagers found that 95 percent of respondents felt at least somewhat happy when expressing gratitude, and over 50 percent felt extremely happy while they were doing so.

Feelings of thankfulness and appreciation have also been shown to contribute to overall health and well-being by stimulating the *parasympathetic nervous system* (the part of our autonomic nervous system that initiates relaxation); this increases levels of immune antibodies, stimulates the release of a beneficial, youth-preserving hormone called *DHEA*, and decreases levels of the stress-related hormone *cortisol*.

But being truly grateful means more than mumbling "thanks" when someone holds a door open or lets you get ahead of him in a supermarket checkout line. It involves cultivating an attitude of gratitude—the beneficial effects of which will be cumulative.

Do you display an attitude of gratitude? Take this quiz and find out.

Take the Test

For each of the following statements, indicate the number of the statement that corresponds to your level of agreement or disagreement:

1. Strongly disagree

2. Somewhat disagree

3. Feel neutral or are not sure

4. Somewhat agree

5. Strongly agree

1. I have a lot to be thankful for.

2. I notice good things in my life even on a bad day.

3. Looking back over my life, I see some experiences that were tough but yielded results I'm now thankful for.

4. I actively count my blessings.

5. I'm reluctant to express gratitude for fear I'll tempt fate to send me some troubles.

6. I take all the credit for my own success.

7. If I made a list of people to whom I am thankful, it would be a long list.

8. I have thanked people face-to-face to whom I feel grateful.

9. I am afraid of looking weak or "uncool" if I openly express gratitude.

10. I keep a gratitude journal, noting things I am thankful for.

11. I never feel satisfied.

12. If I made a list of the good things in my life, it would be long and varied.

13. I often think about things I desire but do not have.

14. I offer prayers of thanks on a regular basis.

15. I envy people who are wealthier than me.

16. I often feel bored and ask, "Is this all there is?"

17. I believe that just the experience of being alive gives us all something to be thankful for.

18. I write notes or letters of thanks.

19. As I get older, I find more and more to be grateful for.

20. If I feel disappointed, I compare myself to others who are less fortunate.

Scoring and Explanation

Before tallying your total points, be sure to *reverse the score* (5 = 1, 4 = 2, 3 = 3, 2 = 4, 1 = 5) *for the following items:* 5, 6, 9, 11, 13, 15, 16. Remember, in reversing the score, high numbers are traded for low and vice versa. Unless you reverse the scores for the items listed—and *only* for the items listed—your result will be inaccurate. See the Introduction to this book for a full explanation of reverse scoring.

Tally your points:

♦ **A score of 85–100** indicates that you display a high degree of gratitude. You take time to thank individuals and to acknowledge powers greater than yourself—whether you call those powers "fate" or "the universe" or the name of a specific deity. You see yourself as part of an interconnected whole, and this conviction brings you a degree of inner peace. The benefits of your thankfulness should accrue and expand over time, and will help you cope with whatever circumstances arise during the course of your life. You are likely to experience a higher magnitude of joy than most people, and even during tough times you will be more philosophical.

♦ **A score of 70–84** indicates that you exhibit a moderate degree of thankfulness. You are certainly not above saying "thank you"— and you sincerely mean it when you do. But you could stand to do it more often and more consistently. (You probably already know this deep down.)

Consider this: once people develop a habitual practice of expressing gratitude, they are inclined to stick with it. In an experiment
known as the "three good things" study (Seligman, Steen, Park,
and Peterson, 2005), participants were asked to take a few minutes
each evening and list three things that went well during their day.
Sixty percent of the subjects in the experiment said they were *still*
ending each day this way, six months after the experiment ended.
To them, the ongoing benefits were obvious.

◆ **A score of 69 or below** suggests that you could do with a much
higher dose of gratitude in your life. As it stands, you may be
experiencing a continual and nagging sense of disappointment and
dissatisfaction. Notice whether you are constantly chasing some
material item that you think will make you happy, only to find
that you quickly adapt to having that item and then crave something else. If this describes you, you are taking a proverbial walk
on what social psychologists call *the hedonic treadmill*—meaning
that you are fruitlessly chasing pleasures that actually don't bring
you much pleasure at all.

Reminding yourself what you have to be grateful for in the
moment can help you quell the urge to jump on that hedonic
treadmill. Imagine how your life might feel different to you if you
stopped, caught your breath, and appreciated all that you already
have—not just in a material sense, but in terms of your strengths,
abilities, and positive relationships.

31

Am I Empathic?

Empathy, a term coined by Sigmund Freud, refers to the ability to identify with others. It involves understanding other people's points of view (different though they may be) and responding appropriately—even compassionately—to their emotional realities. Those who exude empathy tend to be emotionally intelligent across the board. As a result, their relationships prosper at all levels.

Are you empathic? Can you imagine what it's like to walk a mile in someone else's shoes? Take this test and find out.

Take the Test

For each of the following statements, indicate the number of the statement that corresponds to your level of agreement or disagreement:

1. Strongly disagree

2. Somewhat disagree

3. Feel neutral or are not sure

4. Somewhat agree

5. Strongly agree

1. I make it a point to talk to someone who looks lonely.

2. I cry at sad movies.

3. I feel happy when someone I care about is happy.

4. I pay attention to people's tone of voice in addition to their words.

5. I feel envious of other people's successes.

6. I can listen to criticism without being defensive.

7. I can understand someone's politics even if I disagree.

8. I tend to interrupt people when they are talking.

9. I can remember what I felt like at times in my life when I've been blue.

10. I am good at predicting how friends or loved ones will react in any given situation.

11. I have no patience for "whiners" or "cry babies."

12. It makes me happy to watch couples in love.

13. If someone has a phobia, I am sensitive to his fears.

14. I do not poke fun at people if I know they are vulnerable.

15. People should be less emotional and more rational.

16. I choose my words carefully when speaking to someone who is upset.

17. I try to be mindful of how my actions might affect others.

18. I try not to gloat if I have a success.

19. I think everyone is entitled to be irrational sometimes.

20. I tend to carry grudges.

21. I will apologize if I see I have hurt someone's feelings.

22. I will at least smile politely if someone tries to make a good-natured joke.

23. I am good at reading body language.

24. I am very observant of people's facial expressions.

25. Making a mistake doesn't make someone a bad person.

26. I am good at getting shy people to open up and talk.

27. I can find something in common with almost anyone.

28. I socialize only with people who are very much like me.

29. Few issues are all "black" or "white"—I see the nuances.

30. I will end a conversation if someone is going on about herself.

31. I find other people's laughter contagious.

32. Animals have no emotions.

33. I vividly imagine the world of characters in novels.

34. I feel uncomfortable when anyone around me is in a "down" mood.

35. Stereotyping people is unfair.

36. The sound of a crying baby agitates me.

37. I have friends both older and younger than myself.

38. I can't deal with disagreements.

39. I am uncomfortable around people who are ill or who have disabilities.

40. Some people are unfairly judged by the way they look.

41. I would rather avoid someone than give him bad news.

42. I never know what to say on sad occasions.

43. I am comfortable just being silent with someone if that's what she needs.

44. A kind word to someone can make a big difference in her day.

45. I can tell when someone needs to be left alone for a while.

46. I think you should deal with an interpersonal problem immediately, no matter what the circumstances.

47. I would rather just do something for someone than help him do it for himself.

48. Music can alter my mood.

49. I am patient when teaching someone a new skill.

50. I have good timing when it comes to knowing when to raise a subject.

Scoring and Explanation

To obtain the first part of your score, tally your points. But before doing so, be sure to *reverse the score* (5 = 1, 4 = 2, 3 = 3, 2 = 4, 1 = 5) *for the following items:* 5, 8, 11, 15, 20, 28, 30, 32, 34, 36, 38, 39, 41, 42, 46, 47. Remember, in reversing the score, high numbers are traded for low and vice versa. Unless you reverse the scores for the items listed—and *only* for the items listed—your result will be inaccurate. See the Introduction to this book for a full explanation of reverse scoring.

◆ **A score of 151–200** indicates that you are highly empathic. You are capable of sympathetic identification with others. You are very conscious of the fact that other people's realities are as valid as your own, even if they may be informed by vastly different life experiences. Empathy is a desirable trait, but if you are on the very high end of the scale (over 175) there is one caveat: you may feel a lot of pain when you see others suffer. So if you are in a helping profession (say, a nurse or social worker), beware of becoming so wrapped up in other people's problems that you burn out. It's important to take some time away from your work and refresh your perspective. Take care of yourself in addition to caring for others.

◆ **A score of 150 or below** doesn't make you an unfeeling person. You might very well be affable and generous in most situations. However, you might be so wrapped up in your own world that you don't do well at understanding people who are different from you. If you are more willing to pay attention to different points of view, you will learn a great deal about human dynamics and you will end up living a more vivid and textured existence. It all starts with listening more attentively to others.

32

Am I a Cat Person or a Dog Person?

Relating well to people is important, but so is relating to animals. Studies show that people who live with and care for pets tend to have higher levels of well-being than those who do not. Pet owners also tend to have a more positive attitude toward life.

But what kind of pet is right for you? There are over 68 million household dogs and over 73 million household cats in America, making these animals the most common of all pets. But even if you own both—or neither, as of yet—chances are you lean more toward being a "cat person" or a "dog person." Take this quiz to find out about your pet preference, and what it says about you.

Take the Test

For each of the following statements, indicate the letter of the statement with which you agree:

1. I think affection should be given ...

    A. Unconditionally.

    B. Conditionally (given in exchange for caring deeds).

    C. No preference.

2. I consider myself ...

    A. Talkative/gregarious.

    B. Quiet/introspective.

    C. Don't know.

3. When it comes to others' opinions of me, I am ...

    A. Very concerned.

    B. Not especially concerned.

    C. What do you mean—others?

4. I consider myself ...

    A. A joiner.

    B. Independent.

    C. Don't know.

5. On a cold winter evening I like to ...

    A. Take an invigorating walk.

    B. Snuggle by the fire.

    C. Shop online for Florida real estate.

6. When it comes to keeping a schedule, I ...

    A. Am very disciplined.

    B. Opt for spontaneity.

    C. Can't decide.

7. I prefer pets who are ...

    A. Fun to groom.

    B. Self-cleaning.

    C. No opinion.

8. I think a cat's purr sounds like ...

    A. An annoying motorboat engine.

    B. A divine Om-like mantra.

    C. I never heard one.

9. I think puppies ...

    A. Rock.

    B. Smell.

    C. I don't think about puppies.

10. I find kittens ...

    A. Handy, if you like scratched furniture and shredded sweaters.

    B. Precious.

    C. I don't want to find a kitten.

11. I think the reason advertisers put so many golden retrievers in ads is ...

    A. Golden retrievers are so warm and fuzzy.

    B. Cats have too much self-esteem to allow themselves to be exploited by advertisers.

    C. The advertisers could not afford supermodels.

12. I consider myself ...

    A. A very social creature.

    B. Self-sufficient.

    C. Somewhat antisocial.

13. In my opinion …

    A. Cats are too dumb to learn tricks.

    B. Cats are too clever to learn tricks.

    C. I hate tricks.

14. Playing fetch is …

    A. Fun!

    B. Stupid.

    C. What is this "fetch" you speak of?

15. I think ancient Egyptians worshipped cats because …

    A. They were not evolved enough to worship dogs.

    B. They were the most spiritual and intelligent civilization ever.

    C. They did not have *American Idol.*

16. I think hairballs are …

    A. Disgusting.

    B. An occupational hazard.

    C. What's a hairball?

17. I prefer …

    A. Pooper scoopers.

    B. Litter boxes.

    C. I use the bathroom myself.

18. A favorite meal of mine is …

    A. Hamburgers.

    B. Sushi.

    C. Doritos.

19. My favorite style of dress is …

    A. Comfortable and informal.

    B. Elegant and fashionable.

    C. Anything without pet hair on it.

20. I prefer to be awakened by …

    A. Drool and heavy breathing.

    B. Something standing on my chest and kneading it.

    C. An alarm clock.

Scoring and Explanation

Tally your total number of "A" responses, "B" responses, and "C" responses:

◆ **A majority of "A" responses** indicates that you are a dog person. Your partiality for pooches means you want a pet who is emotionally demonstrative, and who is willing to let you exert some control over the relationship (or at least willing to let you *think* that you do). Chances are you also prefer human relationships where the same dynamics occur. You yourself are probably affectionate and outgoing. You do not care too much for surprises, preferring predictability and stability in your life. As for cats, you may find them—and, more importantly, those who prefer them to dogs— hard to fathom. You wonder what people see in pets who are aloof and "above it all." You suspect cat-lovers themselves to be a bit effete, and perhaps not as trustworthy as your fellow dog-lovers.

◆ **A majority of "B" responses** indicates that you are a cat person. Your favoritism toward felines means you are a good match for a pet who is proud and independent—or at least capable of giving you the impression that they are. You don't care as much for a dog's gleeful greetings as you do for a cat's wink and nod when you come in the door. Hey, you don't need a "suck-up" pet to bolster your ego. You know your kitty really adores you—she just plays it cool. When all is said and done they want to curl up with you and purr your praises.

◆ **A fairly even split of "A" and "B" responses** indicates that you are both a dog-lover and a cat-lover. You are truly an equal opportunity pet person who finds lovable qualities in all things fuzzy and furry.

◆ **A majority of "C" responses** indicates that you should get a fish. Or, then again, maybe not.

Part 5

My Money Personality

Money matters are never simple matters. Your relationship to money is intertwined with elements of your personality. In this section of the book, you learn about your tendencies to save, spend, or even splurge. And you discover a lot about the emotions that may underlie your financial decisions.

33

Am I a Spender or a Saver?

Talking about saving money is one of our favorite pastimes. There is no shortage of talk-show segments, books, magazines, and newspaper articles on the subject. But ads that encourage us to part with our money and keep on buying more and more things are ubiquitous. Which way do you tilt? Do you want to pinch every penny—or pitch every penny? Take this quiz and find out.

Take the Test

For each of the following statements, indicate the letter of the statement with which you agree:

1. When I go to the grocery store, I ...

    A. Always shop from a list.

    B. Sometimes have a list, but don't always stick to it.

    C. Buy what I'm hungry for and what looks good.

2. When I get coins as change, I ...

    A. Save them up and cash them in.

    B. Give them to my kids or leave them as a tip.

    C. Leave them in the "take-a-penny" tray.

3. When I clip grocery coupons ...

    A. I make sure to use them on double-coupon day.

    B. I forget I have them and let them expire.

    C. That means Hades will freeze over.

4. If I had to spend some mad money ...

    A. I'd get mad.

    B. I'd spend it on my house or kids.

    C. I'd spend it on myself.

5. I will buy a generic brand of food ...

    A. Whenever I can.

    B. On occasion.

    C. When dogs say "meow" and cats say "woof."

6. I like to pay my bills ...

    A. On time, but not early—I hang on to my pennies until I have to part with them.

    B. By direct debit so I don't have to worry about them.

    C. Not! I'd rather ignore them and buy more stuff.

7. I can tell you how much money is in my checking account …

   A. Within $50.

   B. Within $500.

   C. But I'd be lying.

8. If my 10-year-old dishwasher broke …

   A. I'd try to repair it myself.

   B. I'd call a repairman.

   C. I'd use it as a reason to get a new dishwasher.

9. I have a household budget …

   A. And stick to it faithfully.

   B. But, you know, stuff happens.

   C. Yeah, and I have a unicorn, too.

10. Excluding fast-food restaurants, I dine out …

    A. Less than once a month.

    B. Once a week or so.

    C. Whenever I can.

11. When I go window shopping, I …

    A. Typically buy nothing.

    B. Typically buy something.

    C. Buy everything but the window.

12. I consider anyone who would pay $5 for a latte …

    A. Mentally unstable.

    B. Deserving of an occasional treat.

    C. My best friend.

13. Before buying big-ticket items …

    A. I do extensive research.

    B. I ask my friends what they purchased.

    C. I up my credit card limit.

14. When I plan a vacation ...

    A. I fret about the money I'm spending.

    B. I hunt for some airfare and hotel bargains.

    C. I splurge—Hey, it's a vacation!

15. When I think about retirement ...

    A. I know exactly how much money I will need.

    B. I am a little fuzzy on how much I'll need.

    C. I laugh, or cry.

Scoring and Explanation

Tally your total number of "A" responses, "B" responses, and "C" responses:

◆ **A majority of "A" responses** indicates that you are a saver. You are going to be well prepared for that proverbial rainy day, all right. In many ways, your behavior is admirable. You are prudent and pragmatic—not given to financial whimsy and impulse. But do pay attention to whether your preoccupation with saving is depriving you of the ability to have some fun. Even savers deserve to treat themselves now and then.

◆ **A majority of "B" responses** indicates that you are a mix. You spend a little; you save a bit. This is the most typical set of responses in our society, where most of us are apt to splurge at least now and again. It's okay to do so—if you have the means and if you are also squirreling something away. Could you use a financial tune-up? Sure. Most of us could. Try tracking your spending to see if you can tighten your belt a wee bit without feeling overly deprived.

◆ **A majority of "C" responses** indicates you are a spender. You are good to yourself in material ways, and you have a "can't be bothered" attitude about even simple cost-saving strategies. Although you are a restaurateur's and a retailer's dream, you could be your own worst nightmare. It's time to take yourself in hand—and take your hands out of your pockets.

Do My Emotions Rule My Money?

Many otherwise reasonable and competent people are frightened, seduced, awed, infuriated, or just plain confused by money. This is often because people's reactions to money are based on more personal issues, such as lack of self-worth, than they are on facts and figures. Money is—no pun intended—a very charged matter. But when emotions rule your money, the bottom line suffers.

Do your emotions rule your financial life?

Take the Test

Imagine yourself in the following circumstances and select which of the listed reactions you'd be most likely to have:

1. You've just had a disappointment in love or work and feel sorry for yourself. A friend suggests "retail therapy." You …

    A. Eagerly head off on a shopping spree, buying things on credit that you cannot really afford.

    B. Are way ahead of your friend, having already begun an online shopping binge.

    C. Thank your friend, but suggest another activity the two of you can do together to cheer you up.

2. Your in-laws—who have made it clear they wish you were more financially successful—are coming to a holiday dinner at your house. When you are at their house, they spare no expense on gourmet food and wine. Now you …

    A. Do your best to put out a nice spread without breaking the bank.

    B. Pull out all the stops, calling in a fancy caterer.

    C. Serve a meager meal just for spite.

3. The stock market is dropping fast. You have money in the market in a retirement fund, but you are decades away from retirement. You …

    A. Sell all your stocks.

    B. Do nothing.

    C. Take the time to review your portfolio, with an eye toward staying diverse and perhaps discovering good buying opportunities.

4. A friend who makes a lot more money than you do invites you to an expensive restaurant and picks up the check. You …

   A. Say "thank you."

   B. Say "thank you" and make plans to invite him over for a nice home-cooked meal.

   C. Feel insulted and vow to treat him to an even more expensive restaurant.

5. Your credit card company raises your credit limit without your asking them to. You …

   A. Feel like you just won the lottery and go out to purchase a splurge item.

   B. Ignore it.

   C. Call them and ask them to put it back where it was because you don't want to be tempted to overspend.

6. The price of gasoline is going up, and you fear it will continue to be a long-term strain on your budget. You …

   A. Weigh the pros and cons of investing in a more fuel-efficient car.

   B. Investigate car-pooling options.

   C. Drive miles farther to buy gas that is only pennies cheaper (it's the principle of the thing!).

7. You get a cold call from someone who identifies himself as an investment advisor, and says he can double your money in a month. You …

   A. Send him some money.

   B. Hang up.

   C. Ask him to send you a detailed prospectus.

8. Your car insurance company raises your rates substantially for what you think is an unfair reason. You ...

    A. Shop around for another car insurance company.

    B. Call them and try to negotiate.

    C. Get furious, refuse to pay the bill, and let your insurance lapse.

9. Your rich uncle dies and does not leave you the small fortune you hoped he would. You ...

    A. Feel disappointed, and then get on with your life.

    B. Vow to spend as much time and money as it takes to sue the estate.

    C. Spend a great deal of money on a new car, saying, "Living well is the best revenge."

10. Your spouse or partner says you are spending too much money, and shows you that indeed you are running up household debt. You ...

    A. Figure out ways to hide your personal expenditures from your mate.

    B. Figure out together how you can cut expenses.

    C. Accuse your mate of being a tightwad.

Scoring and Explanation

Match your responses to those noted below. Count up the matches:

1. C. If you picked A or B, you are using money as a temporary feel-good drug.

2. A. If you answered B or C, you are using money to express feelings of low self-worth and resentment.

3. Either B or C is a reasonable choice. If you answered A, you are letting fear rule you.

4. Either A or B is a reasonable choice. If you answered C, you are letting pride rule you.

5. Either B or C is a reasonable choice. If you're not capable of resisting temptation, you can try to eliminate it. If you picked A, you are in denial about the risks of credit.

6. Either A or B is a reasonable choice. If you picked C, you are letting anger rule you.

7. Either B or C is a reasonable choice. If you picked A, you are letting greed rule you and you are prey to pie-in-the-sky thinking. Remember, things that seem too good to be true generally are.

8. Either A or B is a reasonable choice. If you answered C, you are letting indignation lead to your self-defeating behavior.

9. A. If you answered B or C, you are being ruled by false hopes and disappointment.

10. B. If you answered A or C, you are entangling relationship issues with money issues.

♦ **A total of 9 or 10 matches** indicates that you have a rational relationship with money. You tend to make decisions based on factual evidence and logic, regardless of how you feel.

♦ **A total of 7 or 8 matches** indicates that you have an on-again off-again rational relationship with money. Use the answer key to note the particular emotions that are getting in the way of logical decisions, and try to find other ways of dealing with these emotions so that they are not financially destructive.

♦ **A total of 6 or fewer matches** suggests you let your emotional life rule your financial life. This tendency can be extremely costly. Do all you can to be aware of separating your feelings from your finances. Try not to make any financial decisions on a whim, or you risk giving in to your worst impulses. Sleep on everything, and seek solid professional advice when you can.

35

Do I Have Money Envy?

We live in a generally affluent society, where social status—and even presumed happiness—is often equated with observable consumerism. And marketers are intent on perpetuating the idea that we are what we buy and own—or what we wish we could buy and own. Given all this, it's not uncommon for many of us, at least occasionally, to compare our financial state to those of our relations, neighbors, friends, and colleagues.

But if we do this too often, and if we find ourselves coming up short, we may find ourselves contributing to a sense of anxiety and dissatisfaction about our lives. Take the following quiz to find out if you are especially prone to money envy.

Take the Test

For each of the following statements, indicate the number of the statement that corresponds to your level of frequency:

1. Often

2. Sometimes

3. Rarely

4. Never

1. I browse in stores where I know I can't afford anything.

2. If my friends or neighbors purchase something new, I try to find out how much it costs.

3. If my friends or neighbors purchase something new, I get the same thing—or something more expensive.

4. When dining with someone who makes appreciably more money than I do, I insist on picking up the check.

5. I speculate about the salaries of friends, relatives, and co-workers.

6. I buy clothing that I believe will lead people to think I am wealthier than I am.

7. I give more to charity than I can really afford, in order to save face with my peers.

8. When I hear someone won the lottery, I fantasize that it was I who won it.

9. I have taken on debt to give gifts.

10. Not long after I make a purchase, I think about upgrading the item I bought.

11. I like to read or watch TV shows about the lifestyles of the rich.

12. I fantasize about receiving an unexpected inheritance.

13. I spend money I don't have, so that my kids can do what their friends do.

14. I attend "open houses" for real estate that's out of my price range.

15. I can tell you with a high accuracy how much most things cost.

Scoring and Explanation

Tally your points:

◆ **A score of 48–60** indicates that you have a good deal of money envy. You are often preoccupied with thoughts of those who have—or appear to have—more material wealth than you do. And even when you achieve a goal related to acquisition, you are soon dissatisfied with it, and you substitute a new desire for the one you've just satiated. There is a pretty strong chance you equate money with happiness, which is a little ironic because—as you have probably noticed—your infatuation with money and status actually makes you fairly unhappy much of the time.

Your life would be more fulfilling if you stepped off the *social treadmill* and abandoned the idea that you have to keep up with, or surpass, your neighbors, relatives, co-workers, and friends at all costs. Think of the valuable things in your life on which you simply cannot put a price tag. Make a list of those things, and review it each morning and night. Studies show that acknowledging feelings of gratitude for what we do have has a tremendous positive impact in our day-to-day happiness.

◆ **A score of 34–47** indicates that you have a medium degree of money envy. Your envious thoughts don't control your every moment, but they very likely still contribute to a phenomenon known as *social comparison anxiety*—a type of frustration that arises from the fear and displeasure that many people are better off than we are. To temper this anxiety, try comparing yourself to people who have less than you do. Count your blessings—and consider what you might do to help those who are much less fortunate. Altruistic acts are a good antidote for social comparison anxiety.

◆ **A score of 33 or below** indicates that you are largely free of money envy. Sure, you might lust in your heart when you see your neighbor breeze by in a hot new sports car, but chances are the feeling passes after a moment. Overall, you know you can't place a price tag on the things that really count. And you are secure enough not to equate your inner worth with outer trappings.

36

What's My Investment Style?

Each investor favors a certain style of holding onto her money and helping it grow so she can meet her goals. That style has primarily to do with financial risk tolerance. Being familiar with your style of investing can help you make more consistent choices.

Investment style essentially comes down to three different modalities: conservative, moderate, and aggressive. Which one best describes your approach?

Take the Test

Pick the response that most closely mirrors your preference:

1. Which of the following sounds like your investment philosophy?

    A. I never want to lose want I already have.

    B. Slow and steady wins the race.

    C. "Quick" is the best way to get rich.

2. Which of the following would be your most likely criterion for buying a house?

    A. I plan to pay off the mortgage and live in the house for the rest of my life.

    B. It's in a great location for eventual resale.

    C. It's in foreclosure and I can renovate it and flip it.

3. You just inherited $100,000 with the proviso that you must invest it for your children's college education. Which of the following are you most likely to invest it in?

    A. Treasury bills and certificates of deposit.

    B. Mutual funds.

    C. Individual stocks.

4. Would you ever consider buying stock in an IPO?*

    A. What's an IPO?

    B. Probably not.

    C. Yes.

5. Would you ever consider buying a penny stock?

    A. No, but I save pennies in a jar.

    B. Not likely.

    C. Yes.

6. If the stock market dropped 10–15 percent you would …

   A. Feel smug if you owned no stocks, or cash out if you did.

   B. Continue investing the same amount as before each month in mutual funds.

   C. Actively search for undervalued bargains.

7. Your liquid emergency savings would cover your living expenses for …

   A. At least six months.

   B. A month to a couple of months.

   C. What liquid emergency savings?

* An IPO is an initial public offering. It is the first sale of stock by a private company to the public. IPOs are usually issued by smaller, younger companies seeking capital to expand, but might also be offered by large private companies seeking to become publicly traded.

Scoring and Explanation

Tally your number of "A", "B", and "C" responses:

◆ **A majority of "A" responses** indicates that you have a conservative investment style. Your priority is holding on to what you have. You only want to make investments whose value will never dip below where you started. If you are an older investor looking toward imminent retirement, this is a justifiable style. But if you are a younger investor, you might want to explore some moderately risky investments, perhaps pursuing a strategy of investing a steady amount each month in a portfolio of mutual funds. Every investment style has risk—even your conservative style! If you are young and resist any temporary loss at all, you actually risk that all you save could eventually be outpaced by higher costs of living.

◆ **A majority of "B" responses** indicates that you have a moderate investment style. Your priority is steady growth of what you have. You likely own a mix of investments, with some higher risk than others. Although you might well flinch when your investments take a dip, you can grin and bear a bear market by reminding yourself that investments move in cycles.

◆ **A majority of "C" responses** indicates that you have an aggressive investment style. You are at the high end of the risk tolerance spectrum. You are willing to invest higher amounts of money in riskier ventures in the hopes that you will yield far greater returns. You have a strong stomach for market gyrations and are always looking for a way to cash in on any market move.

Note: All three investment styles are valid approaches to investments under certain circumstances. However, it is important to make sure your style matches your goals. To that end, be sure to *define* your goals. Know what you want money *for.* Are you planning for a near-term retirement? That's very different than trying to build an empire as an ambitious 20-something. Be sure to periodically review and revaluate your priorities as you grow older, raise a family, and so on.

37

Am I a Money Waster?

When it comes to wasting money, most of us have a proverbial angel and devil looking over our shoulders. We want to be good, but sometimes, well, we're bad. The question is, how *often* do we waste money? If we're not paying any attention at all to the pennies, the dollars will diminish. Before we know it, they'll have disappeared.

Take the following quiz to see if and when you're spending needlessly, or just plain squandering.

Take the Test

For each of the following statements, indicate the number that corresponds to the level of frequency with which you behave as the statement describes:

---

1. Never

2. Rarely

3. Sometimes

4. Often

---

1. I check my credit card statements to make sure I recognize all charges.

2. I buy store-brand food products rather than advertised brands.

3. I don't count my change.

4. Even if there is a bit of a liquid left in a container, I throw the container away.

5. I have paid sticker price for an automobile.

6. I don't know what my checking account fees are.

7. I bargain at flea markets.

8. I don't check restaurant bills.

9. I track and use my frequent flyer miles.

10. I go to my car dealer for oil changes and other routine maintenance.

11. I keep records of car repairs.

12. I will switch credit cards to get a lower interest rate.

13. I can't be bothered with bargaining.

14. I dry-clean clothing that could be laundered at home.

15. I use the ATM that is most handy, regardless of whether there is a fee.

16. When I give to charity, I do not keep track for taxes.

17. I have no idea how much money I spend each week.

18. I routinely buy coffee out.

19. I will wait for a sale to buy an expensive item I want.

20. I have bought items of clothing I've never worn.

21. I grocery shop when I'm hungry.

22. I have purchased defective items and not bothered to return them.

23. I pick up a "special savings" flyer when I enter a store.

24. I clip coupons.

25. I change printer cartridges as soon as the little light comes on.

26. If there is a sale on meats my family eats, I stock my freezer.

27. If I go to the store for a sale item, I buy other items without checking the price.

28. When the price is right, I stock up on household items I use frequently.

29. If I lend money to a friend, I never ask for it back.

30. I buy commonly used items in large, economy-sized packages.

Scoring and Explanation

Before tallying your total points, be sure to *reverse the score* (4 = 1, 3 = 2, 2 = 3, 1 = 4) *for the following items:* 1, 2, 7, 9, 11, 12, 19, 23, 24, 26, 28, 30. Remember, in reversing the score, high numbers are traded for low and vice versa. Unless you reverse the scores for the items listed— and *only* for the items listed—your result will be inaccurate. See the Introduction to this book for a full explanation of reverse scoring.

Tally your points:

◆ **A score of 90–120** indicates that you waste a large amount of money. You might complain that "time is money" and contend that you can't be bothered counting nickels and dimes. But if you don't do anything to hold on to your hard-earned money, it will continue to slip through your fingers until you find yourself empty-handed. You don't have to rethink all your habits, but try working on just a few as a start.

◆ **A score of 61–89** indicates you are wasting some money. Nevertheless, you also have some sound habits that you can build upon. Remember, every little bit helps!

◆ **A score of 60 or below** means you know how to stretch a dollar. What's more, you probably enjoy getting more bang for your buck. If you're like most people, you will even give in to an occasional splurge. But that's okay. All in all, your strategy should net you many happy returns.

Part **6**

My People-Wise Personality

This section of the book puts your social and emotional intelligence to the test. Are you wise to the motives and agendas of the people with whom you interact? And are you aware of your own internal emotional stumbling blocks? Find out how good you are at intuiting things about others, or if your own moods and attitudes are getting in your way.

Can I Read Body Language?

Body language is an outer map of a person's inner emotions and attitudes. Understanding the gestures, movements, and facial expressions of someone with whom you are interacting offers you invaluable clues as to her thoughts, her evaluation of the situation, and even her opinion of you.

Some people are naturally adept at interpreting body language, and research shows that, in general, women are more skillful at doing so than are men (their ability to decipher nonverbal signals is sometimes chalked up to "women's intuition"). But anyone can learn to be a better "reader." The following assessment will help you evaluate your current level of skill.

Take the Test

Indicate whether you think each statement is TRUE or FALSE:

1. When a person's words conflict with his body language, body language can provide a truer picture of his attitude.

2. It is difficult to "fake" body language for a long period of time.

3. A woman's sideways glance over her shoulder is a "keep away" signal.

4. A "palms up" gesture indicates a willingness to listen.

5. A "palms down" handshake signals a dominant attitude.

6. One or both arms folded across the chest signals a desire to block a threat or any undesirable circumstance.

7. In males, an open-legged stance shows confidence.

8. To create rapport in a handshake, keep your palm vertical and exert the same amount of pressure you receive.

9. Watching where someone places a glass or coffee cup can help you determine whether he is open to you or wishes to create a barrier.

10. The shoulder shrug is a universal gesture indicating, "I don't understand you."

11. Smiling is contagious, and it increases people's positive reactions to you.

12. When a man keeps his hands in his pockets, he is signaling that he wants to have a conversation.

13. Watching how someone uses her hands to sum up a contentious discussion can tell you what side she leans toward.

14. When you want to be persuasive, "steeple" your hands (fingertips lightly touching).

15. Hands held together behind someone's back indicate his sense of superiority.

16. When someone uses his hands to support his head, he is deeply engaged with what you are saying.

17. By briefly touching someone's elbow, you can increase your chances of getting her to cooperate with you.

18. Someone who gives you a double-hand handshake is trying to exert control.

19. When someone rubs her palms together, she signals a negative expectation.

20. People commonly stroke their chins when they are actively making a decision.

21. Displaying your thumbs when the rest of your hands are in your pockets indicates insecurity.

22. Clenched hands during a negotiation indicate that someone is being forthcoming.

23. At a party, you should stand at least 18 inches from someone to whom you are speaking, or he will be uncomfortable.

24. People cross their legs while standing, when they are among those they do not know well.

25. When someone's eyes dart from side to side, he is looking for an escape route.

26. When someone is physically attracted to you, her pupils contract.

27. Straddling a chair with one's legs indicates a dominant attitude.

28. Subtly mirroring someone's gestures can build attraction and rapport.

29. When someone has an opinion she doesn't want to express, she looks down and away.

30. Leaning forward with hands on knees indicates a readiness for action.

Scoring and Explanation

Give yourself one point for each of your answers that match the following answer key:

1. T	9. T	17. T	25. T
2. T	10. T	18. T	26. F
3. F	11. T	19. F	27. T
4. T	12. F	20. T	28. T
5. T	13. T	21. F	29. T
6. T	14. F	22. F	30. T
7. T	15. T	23. T	
8. T	16. F	24. T	

◆ **A score of 25–30** indicates that you are very adept at interpreting body language. Chances are you have always been what psychics call a great *cold reader*—that is, someone who can get an accurate picture of a total stranger very quickly. Maybe you've always thought that you possessed some kind of sixth sense. But you're no Albus Dumbledore, so don't attribute your ability to magical powers. What you possess are keen powers of observation, combined with a deep understanding of human nature.

◆ **A score of 20–24** indicates that you have a respectable degree of ability when it comes to reading body language. If you make it a point to be a bit more observant and read up on nonverbal language (I've listed some great books in the Appendix), you can hone this skill like any other. Then all you'll need to do is learn to trust your instincts.

◆ **A score of 19 or below** indicates that you have a lot to learn about reading body language. You are probably very oriented to verbal communication, but you could be overinvested in words. If you begin to learn about the signals the body sends (see the Appendix for some reading suggestions) and pay attention to them, you will greatly enhance your communications skills and find it easier to build interpersonal rapport.

39

Can I Spot a Liar?

Everyone tells social lies, or little white lies. Such lies are actually niceties that help us negotiate civilized discourse. ("No, honey, you look great in those jeans!") You don't need to be concerned every time someone tells you a polite untruth. But you ought to be alert to occasions when people are actually trying to deceive you in order to cloud your judgment or gain some kind of unfair advantage.

Very often, there are telltale signs when people are trying to pull the wool over your eyes. How much do you know about the ways of the deceitful? Take this quiz and see.

Take the Test

Indicate whether you think each statement is TRUE or FALSE:

1. People tend to touch their noses when they lie.

2. People smile more when they are lying than when they are telling the truth.

3. Words are the least dependable signs of lying.

4. Hiding one's palms while speaking is often a signal that information is being concealed.

5. Rubbing one's finger on the face near the mouth is a sign of lying.

6. It's easier to spot a liar during a phone conversation than in person.

7. People pull at their collars when they suspect they have been caught in a lie.

8. Split-second facial expressions that contradict the person's words are telltale signs of lying.

9. Someone who seems to be trying not to gesture while he speaks may be willfully and skillfully trying to conceal a lie.

10. Most of us tend to believe that attractive people are more truthful than those we find unattractive.

11. Unskilled liars look you straight in the eye, while skillful liars look away.

12. A sudden change of voice tone or pitch often correlates with telling a lie.

13. If you challenge a liar, she will tend to turn the tables and accuse you of lying.

14. If someone is lying and you change the subject, they'll happily go along with you.

15. People speak more slowly when they're lying.

Scoring and Explanation

Give yourself one point for each of your answers that match the following answer key:

1. T	6. F	11. F
2. F	7. T	12. T
3. T	8. T	13. T
4. T	9. T	14. T
5. T	10. T	15. F

◆ **A score of 12–15** indicates that you are great at spotting liars. Hopefully you won't run into too many deceitful types, but if and when you do, you will be ready. It's up to you if you want to call them on their untruths or simply give them enough rope to get caught up in their own tangled webs.

◆ **A score of 8–11** indicates that you can spot some liars some of the time. To begin upping your batting average, note which of your responses were incorrect.

◆ **A score of 7 or below** means you either don't know when people are lying to you or don't want to know. Either way, you could be accused of being a bit naïve. It's fine if you want to think the best of people. Most of them will prove you right most of the time. But try to stay alert to the ways of those who will prove you, on occasion, wrong.

40

Do I Know How to Say "No"?

It's not always easy to say "no"—even when we know that "no" is the appropriate answer. Sometimes people prevail upon us to act against our own best interests. We might agree out of guilt, insecurity, or the desire to please. Or we might agree out of the simple desire to avoid confrontation.

Do you know how to say "no"? It's time to find out.

Take the Test

For each of the following scenarios, note how likely you are to say "yes" or "no." Keep in mind that your "no" can be a *polite* "no." This is not a test of whether or not you are insensitive, but rather of whether you can resist certain kinds of social and emotional pressures when your own needs are at stake.

A. Would likely say "no"

B. Would likely say "yes"

---

1. You are on the telephone with a friend who is going on and on about a romantic break-up. You have many pressing commitments you must attend to. Your friend asks if it's okay to tell you an additional "long story." What do you answer?

2. You are overwhelmed with work when a co-worker you like asks you to help him with a task that is not within your job definition and that he *should* know how to accomplish on his own. What do you say?

3. A family member asks you if he can borrow a substantial sum of money. He still owes you money from the last time he borrowed some, and he has not mentioned the former loan. What do you say?

4. An out-of-town friend asks if it's okay to bring her dog to your house when she comes to visit for the weekend. You are allergic to dogs. What do you say?

5. Your dentist's office calls and asks if they can reschedule your checkup for the next day, as the dentist is rather busy with emergencies. You have developed a toothache and were planning to address it at your checkup. What do you say?

6. You're on a weight-loss diet. Your mother asks you to dinner at her house, and insists that "just this once" you can cheat and have second helpings of her lasagna and homemade chocolate cake, which she made *especially for you*. What do you say?

7. You are good friends with both a husband and wife. One asks you to lie to the other for him so he can avoid an argument. What do you say?

8. Your boss asks you to cover for him at a convention over the weekend after assuring you that you would not have to attend. You have told your family you would take them on a camping trip. What do you say?

9. You are in a rush to get home, but you have to stop at the supermarket for a few items on your way. While in the checkout line, someone asks you if she can "just sneak ahead" with a few things. What do you say?

10. You have chaired a community-based volunteer committee for three years and it has taken a great deal of your time. You have announced your intention to step down and spend more time with your family. Everyone begs you to stay, saying there is no one as qualified as you. What do you say?

Scoring and Explanation

Tally your points:

◆ **If you have three or more "B" responses,** you are not so hot at saying "no."

Granted, most of us can think of a few situations where we are apt to give in to a not-so-reasonable request—perhaps because the consequences of refusal would be more damaging to us than the discomfort or inconvenience of giving in. Most of us can think of a few people who might respond so negatively to our "no" (perhaps for you it is your mother, or your boss) that we'd really rather not antagonize them.

However, three or more "B" answers displays a clear pattern of capitulation that would appear to interfere with your best interests on a regular basis. You are willing to sacrifice a great deal in order to steer clear of taking a stand. You might think of yourself as a "pushover" or a "softie": a real Mr. or Ms. Nice Guy. But others might think of you as a doormat.

Consider the worst that might happen if you took some baby steps toward affirming your boundaries and stating your limitations. Would you survive? Yes. You might step out of your comfort zone for a bit, but you *would* survive. And chances are, you would come to thrive as you took better care of yourself.

Do I Talk Too Much?

Communication is a good thing. But, as with virtually all good things, one can avail oneself of too much of it. Do you talk too much? If you do, you are actually hampering your attempts at communication.

People have limited attention spans. This is especially true in an age as fast-paced as ours and in an environment where many individuals are juggling an unprecedented number of work, family, and community commitments. Even if you are the most fascinating orator in the world (and, no offense, but chances are you're not), busy people will tune you out if you appear to have little respect for their time or little concern for what they have to say.

Is it time to zip your lip? Take this test and see.

Take the Test

For each of the following statements, indicate the number that corresponds to how often you behave as the statement describes:

---

1. Never

2. Rarely

3. Sometimes

4. Often

---

1. I talk more than 60 percent of the time in a conversation.

2. My work presentations tend to go over the allotted time.

3. I am asked to "wrap it up" or "cut to the bottom line" in meetings.

4. I notice people fidgeting when I speak.

5. I have let secrets slip in conversation when I did not mean to.

6. I repeat gossip I have heard, even if I am unsure it is true.

7. I am inclined to share my judgments about other people.

8. I make sure to ask questions of those I am speaking with.

9. At parties, I notice people's eyes darting around the room as I talk with them.

10. I like to impress people with my knowledge of trivia on many subjects.

11. I do nearly all of the talking when I am being interviewed for a job.

12. I actively solicit other people's opinions.

13. During my phone conversations, the other party says he has to hang up first.

14. At work I tend to talk about nonwork matters.

15. I am always interested in what I can learn from other people.

16. I find myself going off on tangents not related to the topic I started to talk about.

17. I have made remarks I wished I could take back.

18. I enjoy telling people what they could do better.

19. When introducing someone, I tell several anecdotes that center on my relationship with them.

20. I share many stories about my private life with people I am not well acquainted with.

Scoring and Explanation

Before tallying your total points, be sure to *reverse the score* (4 = 1, 3 = 2, 2 = 3, 1 = 4) *for the following items:* 8, 12, 15. Remember, in reversing the score, high numbers are traded for low and vice versa. Unless you reverse the scores for the items listed—and *only* for the items listed—your result will be inaccurate. See the Introduction to this book for a full explanation of reverse scoring.

Tally your points:

◆ **A score of 55–80** suggests that you are long-winded. The higher you scored, the more concerned you ought to be. You'll pay a toll for talking too much. At work, your ideas probably won't be taken as seriously as they should. In your personal life, you'll risk alienating friends—or would-be friends—who lack patience for your soliloquies.

Talking is evidently a pleasurable experience for you, and it might serve a functional purpose such as helping you to organize your thoughts. But you should take some conscious steps to curb your enthusiasm.

First, consider the occasion. If time is of the essence, don't say in 200 words what could be said in 20. As the saying goes, "Be bright, be brief, be gone!"

Second, make the most of the limited time you do have. You'll start to lose most people's attention after 20–30 seconds, so get to the point you most want to make as quickly as possible.

Third, remember that listening is an essential part of communicating (see Quiz 43). Don't think monologue; think dialogue! Ask questions. You never know what you might learn when you give someone a chance to answer.

Am I a Narcissist?

A *narcissist* is someone with an extremely high level of self-absorption and a level of entitlement that leads him to focus exclusively on his own needs. The term comes from the Greek myth of Narcissus, a handsome young man so smitten with himself that he fell in love with his own reflection in a pool of water.

We all pass through this developmental phase. In early childhood, we are wholly wrapped up in our own points of view. But as we develop and mature, that self-obsessed perspective is, ideally, replaced by a growing awareness that other people have differing thoughts, beliefs, and feelings that must be taken into account.

Narcissism falls on a continuum. While a healthy threshold of self-regard is desirable, one can be a bit—or a bunch—more self-preoccupied than is desirable to maintain strong and meaningful relationships. Narcissists tend to be insensitive to others and are notoriously bad at respecting social boundaries.

Are you a narcissist?

Take the Test

For each of the following statements, indicate the number of the statement that corresponds to your level of agreement or disagreement:

---

1. Strongly disagree

2. Somewhat disagree

3. Feel neutral or are not sure

4. Somewhat agree

5. Strongly agree

---

1. I feel that exceptions to the rules should be made for me.

2. I have expectations of myself that many see as unrealistic.

3. I fake emotions I think I ought to have but do not actually have.

4. I am immune to flattery.

5. I feel outraged if someone slights or ignores me.

6. I deserve leniency if I do something wrong.

7. I will take on a great deal of debt to make a good impression.

8. Deep down, I know I am an underappreciated genius.

9. I am vain when it comes to my physical appearance.

10. I should be much richer than I am.

11. People have referred to me as "spoiled."

12. I love being the center of attention.

13. I am smarter than most people.

14. People have referred to me as "humble" or "modest."

15. I hate to waste time cleaning up after myself.

16. I believe the universe has something very special in store for me.

17. My time is more valuable than most people's.

18. I have no patience for other people's problems.

19. In conversations, I listen more than I talk.

20. I have no compunctions about attending social events where I am not invited.

21. I have snooped, eavesdropped, or opened other people's mail.

22. I feel like I have psychic abilities.

23. At work, I try to get out of doing menial tasks.

24. In romantic relationships, I fall in love quickly but then cool off quickly.

25. I have ended several romantic relationships abruptly without looking back.

Scoring and Explanation

To obtain your score, tally your points. But before doing so, be sure to *reverse the score* (5 = 1, 4 = 2, 3 = 3, 2 = 4, 1 = 5) *for the following items:* 4, 14, 19. Remember, in reversing the score, high numbers are traded for low and vice versa. Unless you reverse the scores for the items listed—and *only* for the items listed—your result will be inaccurate. See the Introduction to this book for a full explanation of reverse scoring.

◆ **A score of 90–125** indicates that you have narcissistic tendencies. The higher your score, the more these tendencies will tend to undermine you both in relationships and in your ability to achieve the success you so desire.

An excessive preoccupation with yourself can, ironically, be a serious self-defeating behavior. Underneath your veneer of assurance you are extremely vulnerable to criticism and failure, lacking the resources necessary for resilience. And because your actions and attitudes have not led to the creation of a strong social network, you can come up short in the important realm of social support.

Narcissism in its extreme is classified as a type of "personality disorder." But only an individual consultation with a professional can help you discover if you meet such clinical criteria. Also, it's possible to embody some narcissistic traits without meriting a diagnostic label. If you believe you have narcissistic tendencies, make a conscious attempt to consider the needs and points of view of other people. But also be honest with yourself about what your grandiose attitudes *could* be masking. Many professionals who have studied narcissism in great depth contend that narcissists are overcompensating for what actually is self-doubt. Owning up to your own insecurities—we all have them—can be a first step in building a healthier ego and more satisfying and nurturing bonds with others.

43

Am I a Good Listener?

Why listen when you can talk, right? Actually, wrong. Good listening skills translate to good people skills. And the ability to listen carefully and nonjudgmentally results in strong relationships built on trust, tolerance, and understanding. Besides, listening yields knowledge and fresh information that might have otherwise never factored into our decisions. So, all in all, listening benefits us by making us both smarter and more connected to others.

But while listening might seem like a simple enough thing to do, it's quite easy to get distracted or to retreat into one's own little world when others are speaking. Are you a good listener? Here's a chance to find out.

Take the Test

For each of the following statements, indicate the number of the statement that corresponds to your level of agreement or disagreement:

1. Strongly disagree

2. Somewhat disagree

3. Feel neutral or are not sure

4. Somewhat agree

5. Strongly agree

1. I have good audio recall—I can easily repeat information I've heard.

2. People tend to come to me to ask my opinion and seek guidance.

3. I am an impatient person.

4. In school, I'd have the answer when called on.

5. In school, I'd be the one passing notes and watching the clock.

6. I make eye contact with people who are speaking to me.

7. I get fidgety when listening to a speech or presentation.

8. I am well aware of people's emotional tone when they are speaking to me.

9. When someone is being critical of me, I just tune the person out.

10. I can easily paraphrase what someone just said.

11. When someone criticizes me, I rush to defend myself.

12. I rarely have to ask someone to repeat himself.

13. I am aware when people say one thing but really mean another.

14. I can have the radio or TV on for a while and not actually hear what's been said.

15. I really enjoy music.

16. I find most people interesting.

17. I often interrupt when others are speaking—I can't help myself.

18. I am interested in opposing points of view in politics.

19. I often "fake" listening while my thoughts are elsewhere.

20. I ask thoughtful questions.

Scoring and Explanation

Before tallying your total points, be sure to *reverse the score* (5 = 1, 4 = 2, 3 = 3, 2 = 4, 1 = 5) *for the following items:* 3, 5, 7, 9, 11, 14, 17, 19. Remember, in reversing the score, high numbers are traded for low and vice versa. Unless you reverse the scores for the items listed—and *only* for the items listed—your result will be inaccurate. See the Introduction to this book for a full explanation of reverse scoring.

Tally your points:

◆ **A score of 85–100** indicates that you are an excellent listener. You are genuinely interested in what other people have to say, and you value the knowledge you can gain from others. Chances are you are well liked and have strong emotional bonds with others. And odds are high that you make sound, thoughtful decisions based on information rather than on mere knee-jerk emotion.

◆ **A score of 70–84** indicates that you are sometimes a good listener. There are probably situations where you are able to be more patient than others. For example, maybe you can listen well to your partner but tend to zone out in meetings in your workplace. Try applying the skills you use in situations where you listen best to other situations as well. One big listening issue for many is finding it hard to hold our tongues when we are the recipients of criticism. Understandably, we might be more inclined to defend ourselves than to take the criticism in. But if we do the latter, we just might have an "Aha!" moment and learn some things that will serve us well in the future. You won't know until you calm down and pay attention. There will be time to have your say when the speaker has had hers.

◆ **A score of 69 or below** suggests that you do not have much patience for listening. In conversation, you probably spend more time planning what you are going to say next than hearing what someone is saying in the moment. You might be very interested in being understood, but not so very interested in understanding. The thing about listening, however, is that it tends to be a two-way street. If you are willing to genuinely hear and understand others without zoning out, jumping in, or jumping to conclusions, you will find that your point of view gets a fairer hearing.

44

Can I Control My Moods?

We all experience bad moods and negative emotions some of the time. There is nothing wrong with feeling angry or blue for a while. There is a time for everything, but that time must have its limits. If left unexamined and unchecked, bad moods and negative emotions can poison our attitude and outlook, thereby creating a cycle of negativity. But handled with awareness and resolve, bad moods can be put in perspective and we can move on.

Humans and their emotions have been compared to horseback riders and horses. If we ride the "horse" of our emotions, we can rein it in as need be and set our direction afresh. If we let our emotions run wild, they will carry us anywhere and everywhere—like wild horses that refuse to be tamed.

The bottom line when it comes to moods is this: either we take charge of them, or we let them take charge of us. Which is true for you?

Take the Test

For each of the following statements, indicate the number of the statement that corresponds to your level of agreement or disagreement:

---

1. Strongly disagree

2. Somewhat disagree

3. Feel neutral or are not sure

4. Somewhat agree

5. Strongly agree

---

1. When I am sad, I cannot imagine ever being happy again.

2. When I am angry at one person, I take out my anger on others as well.

3. I tend to see situations as black or white.

4. When I am upset, it is impossible to make me laugh.

5. I am good at disputing my irrational fears.

6. People know to stay out of my way when I am in a bad mood.

7. When I am upset, the things I usually enjoy bring me no pleasure.

8. When I am upset, I remind myself that I have overcome difficulties in the past.

9. I eat or drink too much when upset, and then feel bad about doing so.

10. I use exercise, breathing, or meditation to calm myself down when agitated.

11. I am capable of putting a problem aside for a bit while I tend to things that need to get done.

12. I can never sleep when I am worried.

13. A setback in the present makes me think about past setbacks.

14. A disappointment in the present makes me feel hopeless about the future.

15. If I feel rejected by one person, I feel like a complete failure.

16. I never want company when I am upset.

17. I believe even the strongest, most successful people have vulnerabilities.

18. If something doesn't turn out well, I ruminate about what I could or should have done differently.

19. At times I feel unlucky or "star-crossed."

20. When I am in a bad mood, minor irritations cause my temper to flare.

21. I tend to forget my troubles when I am absorbed in my work.

22. I never think to do anything nice for someone else unless I am personally very happy.

23. People have commented on my ability to "bounce back."

24. When I make a mistake, I replay it in my head over and over again.

25. I always say, "Tomorrow's another day."

Scoring and Explanation

To obtain your score, tally your points. But before doing so, be sure to *reverse the score (5 = 1, 4 = 2, 3 = 3, 2 = 4, 1 = 5) for the following items:* 5, 8, 10, 11, 17, 21, 23, 25. Remember, in reversing the score, high numbers are traded for low and vice versa. Unless you reverse the scores for the items listed—and *only* for the items listed—your result will be inaccurate. See the Introduction to this book for a full explanation of reverse scoring.

◆ **A score of 95–125** indicates that you have difficulty controlling your moods. The higher your score, the more you seem to be at the mercy of certain destructive emotions, such as anger or disappointment. You may well have a belief system telling you that you are powerless to regulate your emotions. Perhaps you had role models while you were growing up who seemed to let their bad moods spill into every aspect of their day-to-day lives.

The first step toward gaining power over your emotions is to acknowledge that others like you have consciously and successfully made the transition from "helpless horseman" to "confident rider." The field of cognitive therapy has a vast body of work devoted to the subject and offers techniques such as learning to actively dispute self-defeating thought patterns. In addition, you may want to investigate meditation and other relaxation and stress-reduction techniques.

The best strategy is to find the methods that work best for you. You might actively chart your moods and note what works best to bring you out of a funk. Most of all, remember: you are not helpless. You have the wherewithal to control your moods.

Appendix

Further Reading

Anderson, Peter. *The Complete Idiot's Guide to Body Language*. Indianapolis: Alpha Books, 2004.

Badowski, Roseann. *Managing Up: How to Forge an Effective Relationship With Those Above You*. New York: Currency, 2003.

Berkowitz, Leonard. *Aggression: Its Causes, Consequences and Control*. New York: McGraw Hill, 1992.

Bryant, Fred B. *Savoring: A New Model of Positive Experience*. Mahwah, NJ: Lawrence Erlbaum Associates, 2000.

Civiello, Mary. *Communication Counts: Business Presentations for Busy People*. New York: Wiley, 2008.

Csikszentmihalyi, Mihaly. *Flow: The Psychology of Optimal Experience*. New York: Harper & Row, 1990.

Elgin, Suzette Hayden, Ph.D. *The Gentle Art of Verbal Self-Defense*. Hoboken, NJ: John Wiley & Sons, 1997.

Ford, Charles. *Lies, Lies, Lies! The Psychology of Deceit*. Danvers, MA: American Psychiatric Publishing, 1999.

Glaser, Susan, and Peter Glaser. *Be Quiet, Be Heard: The Paradox of Persuasion*. Eugene, OR: Communications Solutions Publishing, 2006.

Goleman, Daniel. *Emotional Intelligence: Why It Can Matter More Than IQ*. New York: Bantam, 1997.

———. *Destructive Emotions: How Can We Overcome Them?* New York: Bantam, 2003.

Hotchkiss, Sandy. *Why Is It Always About You? The Seven Deadly Sins of Narcissism*. New York: Free Press, 2002.

Howard, Pierce J. *The Owner's Manual for Personality at Work: How the Big Five Personality Traits Affect Your Performance, Communication, Teamwork, Leadership, and Sales*. Austin: Bard Press, 2000.

McAdams, Dan P. *The Person: A New Introduction to Personality Psychology*. New York: Wiley, 2005.

Nettle, Daniel. *Personality: What Makes You the Way You Are?* New York: Oxford University Press, 2007.

O'Connor, Richard, Ph.D. *Undoing Perpetual Stress: The Missing Connection Between Depression, Anxiety, and 21ˢᵗ Century Illness*. New York: Berkley Books, 2005.

Oldham, John M. *The New Personality Self-Portrait: Why You Think, Work, Love and Act the Way You Do*. New York: Bantam, 1995.

Pease, Allan, and Barbara Pease. *The Definitive Book of Body Language*. New York: Bantam, 2004.

Pervin, Lawrence A. *Personality: Theory and Research*. New York: Wiley, 2004.

Post, Stephen, and Jill Neimark. *Why Good Things Happen to Good People*. New York: Broadway Books, 2007.

Provine, Robert R. *Laughter: A Scientific Investigation*. New York: Viking, 2000.

Ridley, Matt. *The Origins of Virtue: Human Instincts and the Evolution of Cooperation*. New York: Viking, 1996.

Seligman, Martin, Ph.D. *Learned Optimism*. New York: Knopf, 1981.

Simon, George K., Ph.D. *In Sheep's Clothing: Understanding and Dealing With Manipulative People*. Little Rock, AR: A. J. Christopher & Co., 1996.

Tavris, Carol. *Anger: The Misunderstood Emotion*. New York: Touchstone, 1989.

Uhl, Arlene Matthews. *The Complete Idiot's Guide to Beating Stress*. Indianapolis: Alpha Books, 2006.

———. *The Complete Idiot's Guide to Dealing With Difficult People*. Indianapolis: Alpha Books, 2007.

———. *The Complete Idiot's Guide to the Psychology of Happiness*. Indianapolis: Alpha Books, 2008.

Wiggins, Jerry S. *The Five-Factor Model of Personality: Theoretical Perspectives*. New York: Guilford Press, 1996.